MW00855996

WHAT YOUR COLLEAGUES ARE SAYING . . .

"Nancy Frey, Douglas Fisher, and Dominique Smith believe that we must nurture ourselves first before we can nurture students and the school: if we do not nurture ourselves, we will have compassion fatigue. Each section of this book supports self-care so that we are prepared to develop a plan for students. This mantra remains true in every chapter. *The Social-Emotional Learning Playbook* will certainly engage teachers while discussing the challenging and important work of improving social-emotional learning within the classroom and community."

—Crystal Wash, Researcher, CERA, Chicago, IL

"Including the social and emotional component in schools is vital, and the relevance of the book is clear: it is designed to be incorporated into a school or district's SEL initiative. The topic is so very important, especially now, after and continuing the recovery after the pandemic."

—Lydia Bagley, Instructional Support Specialist
Cobb County School District, Marietta, GA

"This book is an excellent professional development resource, filled with examples that are culturally relevant and grounded in real-world contexts to help readers understand how SEL can be applied or practiced. I work closely with faculty and students in teacher education and early childhood education programs, and I would recommend this book to them."

—Jeffrey Liew, Professor, Texas A&M University, Bryan, TX

THE
SOCIAL-
EMOTIONAL
LEARNING
PLAYBOOK

THE
SOCIAL-
EMOTIONAL
LEARNING
PLAYBOOK

A GUIDE TO STUDENT
AND TEACHER WELL-BEING

NANCY FREY
DOUGLAS FISHER
DOMINIQUE SMITH

CORWIN

Fisher & Frey

FOR INFORMATION:

Corwin

A SAGE Company

2455 Teller Road

Thousand Oaks, California 91320

(800) 233-9936

www.corwin.com

SAGE Publications Ltd.

1 Oliver's Yard

55 City Road

London EC1Y 1SP

United Kingdom

SAGE Publications India Pvt. Ltd.

B 1/I 1 Mohan Cooperative Industrial Area

Mathura Road, New Delhi 110 044

India

SAGE Publications Asia-Pacific Pte. Ltd.

18 Cross Street #10-10/11/12

China Square Central

Singapore 048423

President: Mike Soules

Vice President and
  Editorial Director: Monica Eckman

Director and Publisher,
  Corwin Classroom: Lisa Luedeke

Associate Content
  Development Editor: Sarah Ross

Editorial Assistant: Nancy Chung

Production Editor: Melanie Birdsall

Typesetter: C&M Digitals (P) Ltd.

Proofreader: Chris Dahlin

Cover Designer: Gail Buschman

Marketing Manager: Deena Meyer

Copyright © 2022 by Corwin Press, Inc.

All rights reserved. Except as permitted by U.S. copyright law, no part of this work may be reproduced or distributed in any form or by any means, or stored in a database or retrieval system, without permission in writing from the publisher.

When forms and sample documents appearing in this work are intended for reproduction, they will be marked as such. Reproduction of their use is authorized for educational use by educators, local school sites, and/or noncommercial or nonprofit entities that have purchased the book.

All third-party trademarks referenced or depicted herein are included solely for the purpose of illustration and are the property of their respective owners. Reference to these trademarks in no way indicates any relationship with, or endorsement by, the trademark owner.

Printed in Canada

ISBN 978-1-0718-8676-2

Library of Congress Control Number: 2022935820

This book is printed on acid-free paper.

22 23 24 25 26 10 9 8 7 6 5 4 3 2 1

DISCLAIMER: This book may direct you to access third-party content via web links, QR codes, or other scannable technologies, which are provided for your reference by the author(s). Corwin makes no guarantee that such third-party content will be available for your use and encourages you to review the terms and conditions of such third-party content. Corwin takes no responsibility and assumes no liability for your use of any third-party content, nor does Corwin approve, sponsor, endorse, verify, or certify such third-party content.

CONTENTS

Visit the companion website at
resources.corwin.com/theselplaybook
for downloadable resources.

ACKNOWLEDGMENTS

Corwin gratefully acknowledges the contributions of the following reviewers:

Jeffrey Liew
Professor
Texas A&M University
Bryan, TX

Crystal Wash
Researcher
CERA
Chicago, IL

INTRODUCTION

Academic learning is impacted by the social and emotional development of young people. In fact, it's impossible to separate social, emotional, and academic learning. Here's an example: a student does not feel a sense of belonging in the classroom. The student's identities are not valued in this place, and the student does not have a lot of coping skills yet. Each of these concerns, individually, will negatively impact the student's academic learning. Taken together, they have a cumulative impact that can prevent learning from occurring.

Importantly, all students need—no, they deserve—opportunities to develop their social, emotional, and academic skills. Social-emotional learning (SEL) is not reserved for students who have already accomplished grade-level learning and need some extra things to do, nor is it an intervention for students who struggle with learning. Social-emotional learning is like any academic subject that students learn in school. Students don't complete the language arts or mathematics standards in elementary school—their learning expands and deepens, year after year. The same is true for social-emotional learning; it should be a given part of the teaching and learning process.

THE CASEL FRAMEWORK

Perhaps the most well-known framework for social-emotional learning in K–12 schools comes from the Collaborative for Academic, Social, and Emotional Learning (CASEL). This multidisciplinary organization began in 1994 at Yale University as a place to name, organize, and implement SEL in partnerships with local school districts. CASEL has grown to be a nonpartisan, nonprofit leader in assisting schools and districts in evaluating social-emotional learning programs, curating research, and informing legislation.

The five-part framework they have developed focuses on the knowledge, skills, and dispositions young people need to learn, reach their aspirations, and be contributing members of their classroom, school, and local communities. Importantly, this doesn't happen in a vacuum. SEL is not something that we "do" to students. You'll note that the CASEL framework contextualizes SEL as interactions at the classroom and school level, as well as with families and caregivers and communities (see Figure 0.1).

FIGURE 0.1 CASEL FRAMEWORK

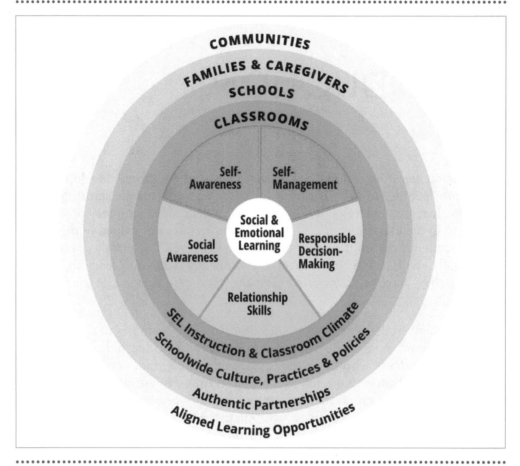

SOURCE: ©2021 CASEL. All rights reserved. https://casel.org/fundamentals-of-sel/what-is-the -casel-framework

So far, so good, right? SEL is a set of skills that operate in a variety of venues. But don't overlook the bottom of the figure. In order to operationalize this, adults must be actively engaged in the effort, through the work they do, to

- Teach skills and promote a classroom climate that fosters dispositions
- Work together at the school level to create a schoolwide culture that manifests the ways these skills and dispositions are enacted through policies, procedures, and interactions
- Partner with families in consequential ways
- Coordinate with communities to create alliances and opportunities for children and adults to thrive

In their 10-year report on intensive SEL efforts across the nation, CASEL found that adult SEL is a key factor in its sustainability (CASEL, 2021). Their reason, they explained, is that when SEL is "interwoven into all adult interactions, it becomes part of the larger culture of the district rather than an initiative relying on a single leader" (p. 26). They asked their district partners to reflect on the previous decade of work they had done, specifically inquiring about what they would have done differently. In retrospect, their district partners noted, "they would have prioritized adult SEL sooner."

The research shows that when teachers tend to their own SEL, it decreases stress levels and increases job satisfaction, which helps them foster warm relationships and better outcomes for students. Adults' personal experience of SEL becomes a powerful catalyst, promoting student and staff well-being, and deepening SEL as an integral part of all district work. (p. 26)

Consistent with CASEL, we view social-emotional learning as a contextualized system of habits, dispositions, knowledge, skills, procedures, and policies that inform the way we work and learn together. Throughout the modules that follow, we will call out specific elements of the CASEL framework to make further connections to the work you do.

TRAUMA AND SEL

Of course, some students have had different experiences that have placed them at increased risk. For example, some students have more adverse childhood experiences (ACEs) than others. These experiences, and the trauma that goes along with them, impact students in profound ways; social-emotional learning, as well as healing and support systems, goes a long way in helping students recover. The Centers for Disease Control developed a conceptual framework as part of the study on adverse childhood experiences represented as a pyramid (see Figure 0.2). They position adverse childhood experiences in the context of their impact on health and well-being.

SEL is like any academic subject that students learn in school. Student learning expands and deepens, year after year.

In terms of the scope of this problem, the CDC study suggests that 61 percent of adults have experienced at least one type of ACE and that one in six people surveyed experienced four or more ACEs. Just under half of the children in the United States have experienced at least one adversity and 10 percent have experienced three or more ACEs (Sacks et al., 2014). Nationally, 61 percent of Black children and 51 percent of Hispanic children have experienced at least one adversity, compared with 40 percent of white children and only 23 percent of Asian children (Murphey & Sacks, 2019). Exposure to ACEs without adequate support leads to prolonged activation of the body's stress response systems. This sustained activation of stress response systems resulting from ACEs has been shown to cause long-term changes in cortisol reactivity and immune function, and to affect the development of brain structures essential for learning and memory (National Scientific Council on the Developing Child, 2014). What, then, are the adverse childhood experiences? The major categories are abuse, neglect, and household dysfunction (see Figure 0.3).

Under the category of abuse, some students suffer physical, emotional, and/or sexual abuse. Of course, these are reportable to the authorities and the system attempts to remove the individual from these situations. But the work is not done there. The impact of abuse lasts, and our collective efforts to help students address the trauma that is associated with abuse are critical to their development. The second category is neglect, which is also reportable but is less likely to receive immediate action from social service agencies unless it is fairly significant and obvious. Like abuse, neglect has lasting effects on the student and our social and emotional well-being efforts can help the student adjust.

FIGURE 0.2 ADVERSE CHILDHOOD EXPERIENCES (ACEs) PYRAMID

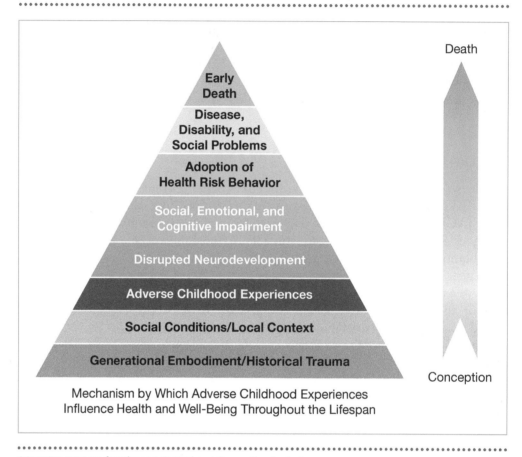

SOURCE: Centers for Disease Control and Prevention (n.d.a.).

FIGURE 0.3 THREE TYPES OF ACEs

ABUSE	NEGLECT	HOUSEHOLD DYSFUNCTION
Physical	Physical	Mental illness
Emotional	Emotional	Incarcerated relative
Sexual		Mother treated violently
		Substance abuse
		Divorce

SOURCE: Copyright 2013. Robert Wood Johnson Foundation. Used with permission from the Robert Wood Johnson Foundation.

The third category of household dysfunction is even less likely to result in attempts to remove the individual from the situation. For example, when a student lives with someone with a mental illness, there is little that social services can do unless the person is harming the child. The same is true for having an incarcerated relative or living through a divorce. Substance abuse concerns are similar; unless the substance abuse is significant or causing neglect, the child is likely to remain in the home living under those conditions. We have lost count of the number of students who report domestic violence in their home but continue to live in that situation because the adult being abused is afraid of reporting to the police, unsure where they would live if action was taken or fearful of retribution if no action was taken. Again, the student is experiencing these adverse experiences that shape their thinking, and without strong social and emotional support and development, these experiences can have lasting and damaging impacts.

If fact, the impact of these adverse childhood experiences is widespread, including decreased educational attainment (e.g., Hardcastle et al., 2018), increased homelessness as an adult (e.g., Herman et al., 1997), increased cases of lung cancer (e.g., Brown et al., 2010), increased prevalence of adult mental illness (e.g., Merrick et al., 2017), and compromised physical health (e.g., Vig et al., 2020). The list could go on, as the impact of ACEs is profound. Ellis and Dietz (2017) suggest that adverse childhood experiences are combined with adverse community environments, creating a pair of ACEs that have profoundly negative impacts on students (see Figure 0.4).

FIGURE 0.4 THE PAIR OF ACEs

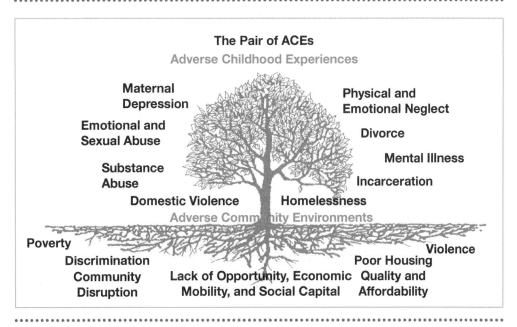

SOURCE: Ellis and Dietz (2017).

The Centers for Disease Control and Prevention (n.d.b.) noted that there are community actions that can prevent ACEs from happening or re-occurring. The CDC suggests that communities should

1. Strengthen economic supports to families
2. Promote social norms that protect against violence and adversity
3. Ensure a strong start for children
4. Teach skills
5. Connect youth to caring adults and activities
6. Intervene to lessen immediate and long-term harms

Of course, as individual educators, we cannot address each of the six recommendations provided by the CDC, but we can help. We can provide a strong start for children, teach them social and emotional skills, connect with our students, and intervene when a student is experiencing abuse or neglect. Specific to schools, Murphey and Sacks (2019) suggest that educators

- Strengthen interpersonal relationships and social and emotional skills
- Support students' physical and mental health needs
- Reduce practices that may cause traumatic stress or retraumatize students

These are the realities of the classroom today, and these realities can cause compassion fatigue. Most of the time, teachers experience compassion satisfaction, which is the pleasure we derive from being able to do our work well (Stamm, 2010). When we feel effective, especially when we see evidence of our students' learning, our compassion satisfaction increases, and we enjoy our work.

> Compassion fatigue is a combination of physical, emotional, and spiritual depletion associated with trauma-related work.

The other side of this coin is compassion fatigue, a combination of physical, emotional, and spiritual depletion associated with the trauma-related work we do where others are in significant emotional pain and/or physical distress. It's known as the high cost of caring. As Figley (2002) notes, "Compassion fatigue is a state experienced by those helping people in distress; it is an extreme state of tension and preoccupation with the suffering of those being helped to the degree that it can create a secondary traumatic stress for the helper" (p. 1435). As Elliott et al. (2018) write,

> Symptoms can develop over a period of years, or after as little as six weeks on the job. Lowered tolerance for frustration, an aversion to working with certain students, and decreased job satisfaction are just a few of the effects that represent a significant risk to job performance as well as to teachers' own personal, emotional, and physical well-being. (p. 29)

The signs of compassion fatigue include

- Isolation
- Emotional outbursts

- Sadness, apathy
- The impulse to rescue anyone in need
- Persistent physical ailments
- Substance abuse
- Hypervigilance or hyperarousal
- Recurring nightmares or flashbacks
- Excessive complaints about colleagues, leadership, and/or those being helped

The effects of compassion fatigue on mental health are also significant and marked by mood disorders, heightened anxiety, relationship problems, difficulty in concentration, and disconnecting from others. It is likely that the overload, the mounting stressors, the lack of attention to how teachers and school leaders are coping with teaching, are triggering more educators to think about leaving the profession. This is the time to recognize and devote the time and resources needed to attend to these issues. We hope that the design of this playbook contributes to that effort.

WHY ISN'T THIS BOOK JUST ABOUT STUDENT SEL?

Consistent with the CASEL framework, you will notice that in each module we start with the self. That means you. For each of the tenets of social-emotional learning we profile in this playbook, we offer evidence-based advice for you and your social and emotional development. Remember, social and emotional learning is a lifelong endeavor, to paraphrase authors Romero et al. (2018) who note in their book about trauma and resilience that "knowing oneself precedes teaching students" (p. 36). You likely have more skills in this area than the students in your classroom or school, but our learning is never done.

We carry trauma with us. As Van der Kolk (2015) noted, "The body keeps score." By that, he meant that traumatic experiences inevitably leave their traces on our minds, emotions, and even on our physical health. We all have those traces, and some of us have yet to address the impact. That's why social-emotional learning needs to continue with adults and should not end upon graduation from high school. In addition, the global pandemic and the increasing understanding of the impact of racism may have challenged some of your social and emotional skills. So, we start with the self.

Social and emotional learning is a lifelong endeavor; our learning is never done.

Each module then moves to our students. For each of the tenets of social-emotional learning, we include ideas for teaching students the skill, whether that be focusing on strengths, building resilience, or regulating emotions. In this section of each module, we provide tools that you can use in your classroom and school to develop this aspect with and for students. In doing so, you will increase your impact on students, both academically and socially.

You will notice that we often provide an effect size. These come from Hattie's Visible Learning® (www.visiblelearningmetax.com), which is a collection of meta-analyses regarding influences on learning. A meta-analysis is a collection of studies that allows for the identification of an overall effect size, or the overall impact of the specific influence. Hattie notes that the average effect size for more than 300 influences on learning is 0.40. Thus, when we report an effect size greater than 0.40, it's an above-average influence on learning. The focus of the Visible Learning database is impact on academic learning, and you will see that many of the topics we address in this book have a direct impact on academic learning. Of course, it's also worthy to note that learning is not limited to academics. As Durlak et al. (2010) noted in their meta-analysis of social-emotional learning, the effect size on social and emotional skills was 0.62. In other words, when teachers teach SEL, students learn. The Durlak study also noted that integrating SEL into the classroom had a moderate impact on academic learning, with an effect size of 0.34. In other words, focusing on SEL is beneficial for students' well-being and does not harm their academic learning, but rather contributes to it.

Finally, each module moves from the self to the students to the school. There are implications for larger groups of people in each of the tenets we discuss. You may not have the authority or ability to implement all the recommendations in the school section of each module. But you can start with a coalition of the willing—colleagues who are interested in their own as well as their students' and colleagues' well-being and social-emotional learning. Perhaps, with your advocacy and support, schoolwide change and implementation can be accomplished.

You'll note a few features in each of the modules. First, you'll see a word cloud based on the contents of that module. Take a look at the terminology, as it is vocabulary we hope you will develop. Having words for concepts is part of the process of learning. and the words allow you to share your thinking and understanding with others. Next, we'll provide some background knowledge on each topic before turning to a vocabulary self-awareness task. This was developed by Goodman (2001) and is useful in monitoring the understanding of specific terms.

> *Only 7 percent of educators surveyed felt prepared to address the social and emotional needs of students.*

From there, we will provide information at the level of self, then students, and then school. In each of these sections, you will find a feature called "Case in Point" that will allow you to analyze a situation and make some decisions. You will note that there are many right ways to think about these cases.

We also include multiple opportunities in each module for you to work alongside the text. This playbook is meant to be interactive. It's meant to be yours. So write in it. Use it to the fullest so that you, your students, and your entire school community benefit.

As noted in a *Forbes* article (Sanders, 2020), only 7 percent of educators surveyed felt prepared to address the social and emotional needs of students. They argue that "SEL can help students better understand and identify their emotions; it can help them develop empathy, increase self-control and manage stress. It also helps them build better relationships and interpersonal skills that will serve them in school and beyond, helping them succeed as adults." We hope that this playbook helps you address the social and emotional needs of students—and, equally important, that it provides you with tools to engage with your colleagues and to continue your social-emotional learning journey.

MODULE 1

BUILDING ON STRENGTHS FOR RESILIENCE

wordclouds.com

BUILDING BACKGROUND

Many of us focus on what we cannot do well and decide if it is worth addressing that need or ignoring it because it will require too much effort to make a difference. This is a common approach in schools. We tend to identify what students cannot do and then focus their time on exactly that. Think about how many data teams and student study teams meetings you've been to that focused only on data about what the student could not do. The result for the student is frustration and can produce deficit thinking in students and teachers. As Waters (2017) notes, focusing on the traits that children and youth do not have can lead them to become disengaged.

> As educators, we use a strengths-based approach when we frame what a young person can do, not solely focus on what they can't do.

There is another way: instead of focusing on what we, or our students, cannot do, we focus on assets. In education, this is known as a strengths-based approach. There is a simple rule in this approach: focus on what students do well. As we will see, that does not mean that we ignore areas of growth, but rather that we build on what students can already do. The evidence suggests that focusing on strengths produces greater levels of happiness and engagement at school and higher levels of academic achievement overall (Waters, 2017). Thus, starting with strengths is good for both academic and social-emotional learning (SEL).

A Strengths-Based Approach

As educators, we use a *strengths-based approach* when we frame what a young person can do, not solely focus on what they can't do. In the words of the Victoria (Australia) Department of Education (2012, p. 6), strengths-spotting teachers look for

- What a child can already do

- What a child can do when provided with educational support

- What a child will one day be able to do

A strengths-based approach is

- Valuing everyone equally and focusing on what the child can do rather than what the child cannot do

- Describing learning and development respectfully and honestly

- Building on a child's abilities within their zones of proximal and potential development

- Acknowledging that people experience difficulties and challenges that need attention and support

- Identifying what is taking place when learning and development are going well so that it may be reproduced, further developed and pedagogy strengthened (p. 7)

Importantly, this does not mean that we turn away from what is difficult, focusing only on the positive and avoiding the truth or minimizing concerns. We do not do ourselves or our students any favors by avoiding discussion of problems and challenges. But we also don't do a young person any good if we focus on what they can't do to the exclusion of everything else. A strengths-based approach assumes that students grow and develop from their strengths and abilities (see Figure 1.1).

FIGURE 1.1 SUMMARY OF A STRENGTHS-BASED APPROACH

A STRENGTHS-BASED APPROACH IS . . .	A STRENGTHS-BASED APPROACH IS *NOT* . . .
• Valuing everyone equally and focusing on what the child can do rather than what the child cannot do • Describing learning and development respectfully and honestly • Building on a child's abilities within their zones of proximal and potential development • Acknowledging that people experience difficulties and challenges that need attention and support • Identifying what is taking place when learning and development go well, so that it may be reproduced, further developed, and strengthened	• Only about "positive" things • A way of avoiding the truth • About accommodating bad behavior • Fixated on problems • About minimizing concerns • One-sided • A tool to label individuals

SOURCE: Victoria Department of Education and Early Childhood Development (2012, p. 9)

Deficit thinking fills the void when a strengths-based approach is absent. This "blame the victim" view focuses attention on internal deficiencies which might be "cognitive, behavioral, motivational or contextual in nature" (Kennedy & Soutullo, 2018, p. 12). Deficit thinking about students contributes to an "exoneration of educator responsibility" by instead saying, "We can't fix that" (p. 11). Deficit thinking is manifested in several ways, as Valencia (2010) described:

> *Deficit thinking about students contributes to an "exoneration of educator responsibility" by instead saying, "We can't fix that."*

1. **Victim blaming:** Considering the student's personal characteristics (race, ethnicity, language proficiency, socioeconomic status) as the cause

2. **Temporal changes:** Blaming the context, such as home or culture, for the problem

3. **Educability:** Believing that a student can't learn (e.g., "I tried all these different strategies, and nothing works")

4. **Pseudoscience:** Falsely attributing evidence obtained or interpreted using a deficit lens (e.g., using a behavior log to encourage punishment at home)

5. **Oppression:** Instituting policies that disadvantage some students, such as remedial classes and zero-tolerance suspension and expulsion policies

6. **Orthodoxy:** Preserving institutional policies because of a lack of will to try something new (e.g., "All misbehaving students go to the dean of students because that's the way we've always done it")

Black and Latinx students, students with disabilities, unhoused children, and foster youth are placed at high risk in classrooms and schools that perpetuate deficit thinking as a way of doing business. The statistics on suspension and expulsion rates are disproportionate compared to their representation in schools, which in turn impacts their school attendance. And it's really difficult to improve the academic and social-emotional lives of young people when they're not there, don't you think? At a time when educators are reporting mounting concerns about the state of students' mental well-being, we cannot afford to have students needlessly spending more time away from us. It is imperative that we actively adopt a strengths-based approach for all students.

Self-Determination

A fundamental principle in the education sciences is that we teach by using a learner's prior knowledge to bridge to new knowledge. It doesn't make sense to have a child solve multiplication problems, for instance, when they don't have a good grounding in addition. Now imagine that the same child is told to do the multiplication problems but doesn't receive much in the way of teaching and scaffolding to solve them. It would be discouraging for the learner and frustrating for the teacher. In fact, it would likely result in *unproductive failure*, the term Kapur (2016) uses to describe unguided problem solving.

And yet, too often, we expect ourselves, our students, and our schools to tackle a situation for which there is little prior knowledge and not much of a guide for how to achieve a goal. A very wise adult with a disability described his experience as a student who spent years in segregated special education classrooms: "It's where you go all day long to do things you're not good at." His experience was that there was little interest in what his strengths were (he was an amazing mathematician and computer coder); instead, there was a narrow focus on what he couldn't do well (in his case, communication, social interactions, and managing his emotions were challenges).

> *Self-determination is expressed as a mindset that seeks to improve the lives of people, not just ease suffering.*

Such experiences have led to important shifts in approaches to special education, particularly in *self-determination theory*, which relies on three dimensions: autonomy, competence, and relatedness (Ryan & Deci, 2000). The authors note that "human beings can be proactive and engaged or, alternatively, passive and alienated, largely as a function of the social conditions in which they develop and function" (p. 68). In other words, when these conditions are present, motivation increases. Consider what we know about what works for ourselves, our students, and our organization:

- **Autonomy** to make choices and decisions, which contributes to a sense of agency to achieve goals

- **Competence** to demonstrate skills and develop new ones

- **Relatedness** to others through social bonding such that one doesn't feel alone

Self-determination is expressed as a mindset, adopted by professionals, that seeks to improve the lives of people, not just ease suffering. It is a motivational tool used in a wide array of fields outside of education, from smoking-cessation programs to athletic coaching efforts. One recent innovative application was a university's redesign of its financial advising (Angus, 2020). The counselors recognized that the effects of COVID-19 were threatening the financial well-being and mental health of their students and sought to use a strengths-based approach to assist students in "acknowledging past achievements and encourage and build greater self-determination and a sustainable financial future" (p. 96). By using this approach, counselors found that university students were more likely to utilize resources available to them and reported decreased levels of anxiety.

Self-determination is crucial for building resilience in the face of adversity. *Resiliency* is a measure of the ability to adapt to change, especially when that change is prompted by loss, unexpected problems, distress, trauma, and other adverse events. One's resilience is not a function of personality, which is very good news; it is a strength that can be cultivated. Your emotional intelligence is central, as is knowing about your strengths and being able to cognitively reframe situations to better understand them. Resilience is enhanced when there is a sense of belonging and affiliation to the group, which can be a source of comfort and guidance. Emotional regulation plays an equally important role, especially in recognizing feelings and using calming techniques to maintain equilibrium. Whether we are six years old or 36 years old, investment in these qualities is an investment in the resilience each of us needs.

> *We are better able to apply a strengths-based approach to our students and engage in self-determination if we are also doing so internally for ourselves.*

We are better able to apply a strengths-based approach to our students and engage in self-determination if we are also doing so internally for ourselves and at the institutional level as schools.

In this module, we will explore three dimensions of a strengths-based approach, and you will learn

- How to find and cultivate your own strengths and recognize them in others

- Ways to promote student strengths by understanding their assets and leveraging their strengths for students you find challenging

- How to maximize a strengths-based approach at the school level to develop its social capital and resiliency as an organization

VOCABULARY SELF-AWARENESS

Directions: Consider the terms below.

- If it is new to you, write the date in the Level 1 column.

- If you have heard the word before but are not sure that you can use it in a sentence or define it, write the date in the Level 2 column.

- If this word is very familiar to you and you can define it and use it in a sentence, write the date in the Level 3 column.

Update your understanding of the terms as you engage in this module and in your work. Note that there are spaces for you to add terms that are new to you.

WORD	LEVEL 1	LEVEL 2	LEVEL 3	SENTENCE	DEFINITION
Strengths-based approach					
Self-determination theory					
Resilience					
Deficit thinking					
Cognitive reframing					
Character strengths					

WORD	LEVEL 1	LEVEL 2	LEVEL 3	SENTENCE	DEFINITION
Stereotype threat					
Asset mapping					
Social capital					

....

Level 1 = This word is new to me.

Level 2 = I have heard this word before.

Level 3 = I know the definition and I can use it in a sentence!

CASEL Connections for educators, students, and schools in this module:

SELF-AWARENESS	SELF-MANAGEMENT	SOCIAL AWARENESS	RELATIONSHIP SKILLS	RESPONSIBLE DECISION MAKING
Knowledge of strengths	Resilience Cognitive reframing		Social capital	Self-determination

USING STRENGTHS BEGINS WITH SELF

"It's not me. I have amazing people around me."

We have likely heard or uttered a sentiment like the one above before. Someone is praised for an accomplishment, and they attribute their success to those around them. Is that a strength or a weakness? The answer is: It depends. It may be a weakness for that person if they go on to attribute their accomplishment to luck and have difficulty in accepting a compliment. But it may well be evidence of a character strength; in this case, humility. Couple that with a strength in teamwork, and that person may very well be a valuable colleague who contributes to the collective responsibility of a school.

A strengths-based approach begins with identifying one's own in order to leverage them and to work around other dimensions of oneself that are lesser strengths. There is good evidence that self-knowledge, which is to say knowing, naming, and leveraging one's strengths, contributes significantly to one's confidence, life satisfaction, and the quality of personal and professional relationships (Schutte & Malouff, 2019).

Character strengths research has been conducted for the last 20 years. Utilizing the positive psychology research pioneered by Martin Seligman, past president of the American Psychological Association, and Mihaly Csikszentmihalyi, best known for his ground-breaking work on the flow state, several validated instruments have been developed to help people identify their strengths. The best known of these is the Values in Action Inventory of Strengths (VIA-IS; see Figure 1.2) that organizes 24 core human strengths into six virtues (Peterson et al., 2005). These are not emotions, which are situational and change frequently, but rather personality traits that persist over time. Validity and reliability studies have demonstrated that the instrument has a strong test-retest, meaning that results for an individual are stable over a period and that the items accurately assess the traits. You can learn more about each of these core human strengths by viewing brief descriptions of each at https://www.viacharacter.org/character-strengths.

FIGURE 1.2 VIA-IS CHARACTER TRAITS AND VIRTUES

	CHARACTER TRAITS				
VIRTUE 1: WISDOM	Creativity	Curiosity	Judgment	Love of Learning	Perspective
VIRTUE 2: COURAGE	Bravery	Perseverance	Honesty	Zest	
VIRTUE 3: HUMANITY	Love	Kindness	Social Intelligence		
VIRTUE 4: JUSTICE	Teamwork	Fairness	Leadership		
VIRTUE 5: TEMPERANCE	Forgiveness	Humility	Prudence	Self-Regulation	
VIRTUE 6: TRANSCENDENCE	Appreciation of Beauty and Excellence	Gratitude	Hope	Humor	Spirituality

SOURCE: © Copyright 2004–2022, VIA Institute on Character (n.d.). All rights reserved. Used with permission. www.viacharacter.org

We invite you to pause at this point in the playbook to learn about your own strengths. Go to https://www.viacharacter.org to take this free online version of the VIA-IS. Once you set up an account, you can take the 240-item assessment. We know that sounds daunting; it will take you less than 15 minutes. It consists of statements that you rate on a scale of 1 to 5, with 1 being *This is very much unlike me* to 5 being *This is very much like me*. Examples of statements follow:

- I know that I will succeed with the goals I set for myself. (Hope)

- I always treat people fairly, whether I like them or not. (Fairness)

- At least once a day, I stop and count my blessings. (Gratitude)

Once completed, you will immediately receive a short report of your strengths in numerical order, beginning with your signature strengths, then your middle strengths, and finally, your lesser strengths. We promise that this is not a magazine-style quiz. This instrument is widely used and appears in the *Psychologists' Desk Reference*.

After you receive your results, reflect on what you have learned about yourself and your signature strengths.

What was surprising to you?	What was confirming for you?

INVEST IN YOUR STRENGTHS TO BUILD RESILIENCE

Knowing one's strengths and being intentional about using them contributes to your own ability to achieve your personal and professional goals. Once again, keep in mind that your lesser strengths are not deficits, but rather ones that you use less frequently. If there are some you want to cultivate, go for it. One of the important findings of character strengths research is that strengths and weaknesses are not fixed nor are they biologically based—they can be developed with intention. Keep in mind that your signature strengths also offer a pathway for you to grow and develop. They are key to your personal and professional resilience.

> Character strengths research shows that strengths and weaknesses are not fixed. They can be developed with intention.

Being knowledgeable about yourself contributes to your resilience, especially when it makes it possible to consciously draw on the strengths you have to navigate unsteady times. Misfortunes and setbacks happen, and being resilient will not prevent their occurrence. However, resiliency impacts your ability to handle adverse events and the changes that result. Change can also be the impetus for innovation. However, change is difficult and sometimes uninvited, although it can result in unexpected possibilities. Most of us don't crave change, even though we know it can be necessary. Our colleague Cathy Lassiter reminds us of this when she says, "Change is good. You go first." To be sure, pandemic teaching, as one example, has profoundly changed the ways schools function, from logistics and scheduling to the ways we interact with students, colleagues, and families. But as Aguilar wisely writes, "We know the key to resilience is learning how to get back to the surface when a ferocious wave knocks us over, how to ride those waves, and perhaps, even how to find joy when surfing the waves" (2018, p. 268).

CASE IN POINT

Hannah Pritchard-Jones teaches sixth-grade social studies at the same school she attended as a student. She regards this as her dream job, especially because this is her first year of full-time teaching. Her university preparation program occurred in another district during an extended period of full-time distance learning, so she didn't have the same experiences as other student teachers in previous years have had. She's a few months into her first experience teaching in a physical classroom, and, frankly, she's overwhelmed. There's a different level of classroom management required, and she's feeling unsure of how to ask for help, fearing that it might be seen as a sign of weakness. All her frustrations and anxieties reach a tipping point during a conversation with the induction coach: in tears, Ms. Pritchard-Jones confesses that she's feeling like she is not cut out for teaching. She does admit that the best part of her job is the relationships she has built with many of her students.

The instructional coach sees that this novice teacher is at a crossroads and wants to shape her perspective by building a sense of self-determination, as she knows this will contribute to Ms. Pritchard-Jones's resiliency. What recommendations would you give to the induction coach and the teacher in each of these areas?

AUTONOMY	COMPETENCE	RELATEDNESS

A STRENGTHS-BASED APPROACH CONTINUES WITH STUDENTS

Learners who work from a position of strength are more likely to learn faster and more completely (Clifton & Harter, 2003). In addition to improved academic performance, students in this mode report having feelings of mastery and accomplishment and are motivated to take on new challenges. This is at the center of definitions of a visible learner. Of course, visible learners don't just happen by chance. They are built by educators who create the conditions such that the teacher is able to see learning through the eyes of their students (Hattie, 2012).

> Learners who work from a position of strength are more likely to learn faster and more completely.

Many of the conditions consistent with Visible Learning intersect with dimensions of autonomy, competence, and relatedness. A strengths-based approach to learning enhances each of these: For instance,

- Creating opportunities for choice and decision making about consequential matters in the classroom is a strengths-based approach to autonomy.

- Student competence is enhanced through culturally sustaining curricula that allow students to draw on their cultural and linguistic knowledge (Paris & Alim, 2017).

- Social relatedness is developed more fully when students are provided lots of chances to work with one another and learn about themselves.

We find that it's of great importance to build the collective efficacy of student teams. Equipping teams with decision-making responsibilities about how they will work together and providing instruction about the social skills needed for collaboration can assist in this effort (Hattie et al., 2021).

INVEST IN YOUR STUDENTS AS ASSETS

Being a strength-spotter for your students requires that you know a lot about what they bring to the classroom. These assets, which include family, culture, and experiences, provide individuals with unique strengths. Caring educators will tell you that no two years are the same in their classrooms, even when they are teaching at the same grade level or subject. That's because each year students bring their distinctive selves and therefore shape the dynamic of the room. In the words of Style (2014), "half the curriculum walks in the room with the students, in the textbooks of their lives" (p. 67). She notes that for too many young people, the shelves don't reflect the lives of the students.

Now let's link this to a concept we will focus on more deeply in the next module—belonging. In classrooms and schools where a sense of belonging is diminished for some students, and where what is learned in the classroom doesn't fit into their lives, there is fertile ground for stereotype threat to take root. *Stereotype threat* is "the threat of confirming or being judged by a negative societal stereotype . . . about [a] group's intellectual ability and competence"

(Steele & Aronson, 1995, p. 797). It is believed that stereotype threat has an unfavorable effect on memory and attention and therefore interferes with academic performance. Black students are particularly vulnerable to stereotype threat, yet it has been documented among Latinx, Asian-American students, female students in mathematics and science classes, and people with disabilities. With an effect size of −0.29, it is one of the negative influences on student learning (www.visiblelearningmetax.com).

An assets-based approach to curriculum development can serve as something of a counterbalance to stereotype threat. It may begin with seeking out ways to profile contributors to the discipline you teach beyond the conventional ones featured in the textbook. And of course, make sure that the narrative and informational texts in your classroom reflect the heritages of your students. But go beyond the general demographics of your classroom and ask yourself, "Do I really know my students as individuals?" If the answer is "Not as much as I should," take a look at asset mapping.

> *Being a strength-spotter for your students requires that you know a lot about what they bring to the classroom.*

Asset mapping is a student-generated visual representation of the cultural strengths and community resources they draw on (Borrero & Sanchez, 2017). It's likely that you have seen asset maps in other contexts, such as an illustrated map of a city that highlights attractions like museums, parks, and libraries. Think of your students' lives much like a city.

Students use inquiry to discover stories about their families, identify individual strengths, and draw on the values and ideals of the community in which they live. These asset maps are displayed and used for a classroom gallery walk. A second gallery walk is hosted to invite families and community members to see the assets their children have identified.

As one example, Samoan American high school students identified generosity, family responsibility, and respect as important cultural traditions that sustained them from one generation to the next in their efforts to combat the effects of systemic racism (Yeh et al., 2014). Now consider how these cultural assets could be leveraged by their teachers. *Generosity* is a necessary condition for high levels of collaborative learning to occur. Values of *family responsibility* can be utilized to empower young people to name and work toward college and career aspirations that benefit their families. And *respect* illuminates the importance of conveying unconditional positive regard for a student. Knowing your students' cultural assets (and using these assets) increases your effectiveness. Students' knowledge of their cultural assets helps them discover their power.

Younger students will likely respond well to questions that encourage them to find out more about their family's history, develop timelines of their own life, and identify places and traditions that are important to them. Useful questions might include the following:

- Who helps you?

- What do you know about your culture?

- Who can help you understand your culture?

- What traditions are important in your family?
- What traditions are important in your community?

Older students can add more about historical experiences that have shaped their ancestors' lives, identify local community leaders and institutions they value, and report on their own advocacy and service. For example, adolescents might want to share the struggles they have experienced, the issues that they care about in society, and the ways in which their ancestors have shaped their life.

NOTE TO SELF

Consider how you might use asset mapping in your classroom or across the school.

With whom might you use asset mapping?	
How might it enhance a unit of instruction?	
What are the benefits you could gain by doing so?	
What resources (e.g., community partnerships, family collaboration) do you have to do so?	
What resources do you need to do so?	

INVEST IN YOUR STUDENTS' ABILITY
TO LEARN ABOUT THEIR STRENGTHS

An asset-mapping project can provide students with a window to see that what they bring to the classroom is valued and respected. Continue that conversation by ensuring that students are able to learn about their own strengths that they possess as individuals. As we discussed in the previous section, the VIA-IS is a tool grounded in the research about character strengths. There is also an online version for students ages 8 through 17 to use in order to identify their signature strengths. The online tool for young people consists of 103 questions and takes 10 to 15 minutes to complete. The questions are further adjusted by age to improve readability for younger students and can be accessed at https://www .viacharacter.org/surveys/takesurvey.

It is important for families to see the strengths their child possesses. Families with a child with a history of school failure may have lower expectations because they have not experienced their child's successes. Make sure that your interactions with families include highlights of their child's contributions. Far too often, families report that the only time they hear from the school is when their child is having a problem, often behavioral. Interrupt this cycle by committing to reaching out to the families of every child on your roster regularly to discuss a strength you see, and more often for students who have a history of difficulty. This may come in the form of a short note, phone call, or text. Most schools use a student management information system (MIS) to manage gradebooks, and these systems are accessible by parents. Add a field to the MIS that allows you to add strengths-based comments for families to read.

> *Students' knowledge of their cultural assets helps them discover their power.*

Family interactions often come in the form of parent-teacher conferences. We are fans of a series of questions that can be posed to the child and their family to focus attention on their strengths. We have used similar questions during summer home visits conducted by special educators for incoming ninth-grade students at the school where we work. These questions come from Your Therapy Source (2019), which profiles resources for pediatric therapists, educators, and parents:

1. This student is best at . . .
2. This student has an amazing ability to . . .
3. This student is frequently recognized for . . .
4. This student smiles when . . .
5. This student is happiest when . . .
6. This student participates the most when . . .
7. This student does this better than any other student . . .
8. This student is highly interested in . . .
9. This student is highly motivated by . . .
10. This student always takes pride in their work when . . .

Being a strength-spotter requires deliberate intention to do so. All of us have been caught up at one time or another with a script that seems more intent on cataloging everything that is wrong without giving attention to what is working, and what strengths that young person possesses. Often, tapping into their strengths is key to changing their learning trajectory.

NOTE TO SELF

Now it's your turn. It's easy to talk about a strengths-based approach in a theoretical way, but more challenging when we're talking about *that kid*. You know, the one that keeps you awake at night as you struggle to make a breakthrough. That child who frustrates you. That young person who causes you to dread third period because you know they came to school today, and you wish they hadn't. Now that you've got that current student in your mind, respond to the following prompts.

1. This student is best at . . .

2. This student has an amazing ability to . . .

3. This student is frequently recognized for . . .

4. This student smiles when . . .

5. This student is happiest when . . .

6. This student participates the most when . . .

7. This student does this better than any other student . . .

8. This student is highly interested in . . .

9. This student is highly motivated by . . .

10. This student always takes pride in their work when . . .

If you are at a loss to answer any of these questions, then it's a signal that you need to learn more about the student. If you were successful in answering these questions as positives, consider how you are going to leverage these strengths.

CASE IN POINT

The preschool educators at Rockdale Community School are meeting to hone their skills at developing strengths-based plans for their young students. The preschool is inclusive of children with and without disabilities, a practice endorsed by the National Association for the Education of Young Children (Barton & Smith, 2015). They are working through three scenarios based on children in their charge to shift to a strengths-based approach. Help them rewrite these statements using your knowledge of strengths. To prepare you for this, reread the chart in Figure 1.1 on what a strengths-based approach is and is not.

(Continued)

(Continued)

DEFICIT-BASED STATEMENT	STRENGTHS-BASED TEACHING STATEMENT
Madison has difficulty transitioning to the classroom in the morning and it takes her a long time to settle down.	
Carlos is an English learner and can't communicate his needs in English to his teachers.	
Karina hits and grabs other children to get their attention.	

A STRENGTHS-BASED APPROACH IS NURTURED BY SCHOOLS

Is your school currently leveraging its strengths? The organization of traditional schools often resembles silos, with adults working hard within a particular department or job assignment but with little contact across other sections. The result is that at times, the adults in the school are working at cross purposes from one another. This isn't intended but what can happen when the work of the school is subdivided and individual units take their place. It isn't necessarily a matter of the size of the school. We've seen large high schools that serve 2,000-plus students where there is a cohesive mission and small schools of 200 students that seem to operate in different zones within the building.

SOCIAL CAPITAL OF SCHOOL IS STRENGTH BASED

An untapped source of strength in schools is its social capital. *Social capital*, which is derived from economics, describes the ways that groups invest in each other. Instead of money, the investment is in the relationships with one another. Importantly, these networks extend to their relationships with the community. The social capital of a school is a product of a shared mission, its values, and its norms. It is an intangible that is deeply linked to the achievement of its students.

A well-known example of social capital at work was profiled by the Chicago Consortium of School Research. They studied 100 elementary schools in the district to determine what made some schools successful while others were less so, with controls for things like demographics and the socioeconomic status of the neighborhood. The results they reported were striking. They found that the relative social capital of a school, which is to say the network of relationships in the building and with the community, was predictive of the academic achievement of its students and in measures of school safety (Bryk, 2010). And it makes a lot of sense. A child in a school community with high levels of social capital sees allies and supporters in and out of school. In turn, that child is seen as an individual with strengths.

High schools run in large part on social capital, even though they might not be aware of it. It turns out that social capital is predictive of graduation rates, reading scores, and math scores. Salloum and colleagues (2017) examined social capital at 96 high schools. They found that four characteristics mattered:

- The normative behaviors of the school (how problems are resolved, and decisions are made)

- Relational networks (the triangle of interpersonal relationships between teachers, students, and their families)

- Trust in parents (the belief of school staff that parents and teachers work together effectively to achieve goals)

- Trust in students (the belief of school staff that students work together with teachers effectively to achieve goals)

Much like the elementary schools study, the socioeconomic status of these high schools was not predictive of social capital. In fact, there were well-resourced schools that had low social capital. The researchers reported that "in our study, schools with stronger reports of connecting teachers, parents, and students had higher average levels of achievement" (Salloum et al., 2017, p. 20).

Understanding the assets that families and communities possess makes it possible to trade on them for the benefit of students.

Schools with high social capital promote and leverage the strengths of their members. Students are viewed as individuals who each bring their own strength profile to school. Adults who work at the school understand their strengths and recognize them in others. Communities are viewed as assets, not problems to be fixed. It is the frequent interactions between these actors—teachers, students, and families—that foster the social capital of the school. Recognition of one's own strengths, as well as those our students possess, is foundational to meaningful relationships. And understanding the assets that families and communities possess makes it possible to trade on them for the benefit of students.

NOTE TO SELF

Do you know your school's social capital? Begin with a survey of school staff using the social capital scale in Figure 1.3 (of course, this can be translated or delivered using text-to-speech tools). After tabulating the results, look at the relative amount of social capital distributed among students, families, and the community. If you find that there are low levels, investment in a strengths-based view of learners and their communities may be a great way to raise the quality of the network of relationships at your school.

FIGURE 1.3 SOCIAL CAPITAL SCALE

SOCIAL CAPITAL SCALE ITEMS	STRONGLY DISAGREE					STRONGLY AGREE
Teachers in this school have frequent contact with parents.	1	2	3	4	5	6
Parental involvement supports learning here.	1	2	3	4	5	6
Community involvement facilitates learning here.	1	2	3	4	5	6
Parents in this school are reliable in their commitments.	1	2	3	4	5	6
Teachers in this school trust the parents.	1	2	3	4	5	6
Teachers in this school trust their students.	1	2	3	4	5	6

SOCIAL CAPITAL SCALE ITEMS	STRONGLY DISAGREE					STRONGLY AGREE
Students in this school can be counted on to do their work.	1	2	3	4	5	6
Students are caring toward one another.	1	2	3	4	5	6
Parents of students in this school encourage good habits of schooling.	1	2	3	4	5	6
Students respect others who get good grades.	1	2	3	4	5	6
The learning environment here is orderly and serious.	1	2	3	4	5	6

SOURCE: Goddard (2003, p. 71). Used with permission.

COGNITIVE REFRAMING BUILDS ORGANIZATIONAL RESILIENCE

Care and compassion require that we feel the other person's needs and then take actions to help. A tool for doing so is called *cognitive reframing*. It is natural when an event occurs to consider it first through its impact on us; to put it another way, we frame the event through our own lens. One example is the well-known phenomenon of recalling exactly where we were and what we were doing when a traumatic event took place. You might recall what was happening the moment you heard about a space shuttle explosion or an assassination of a political leader. While we were not personally involved in the incident, we initially focus on the situation as something that happened to ourselves. The many events and situations that occur in our professional lives rarely, if ever, rise to the level of extreme trauma. We offer this as an example of the natural tendency to process events emotionally.

Now consider an event that occurs far more often at our professional levels, such as a simmering dispute with another colleague. It's fairly low level, but it troubles us. It is quite possible that it has led us to overgeneralize, like the examples that follow.

- It happened once before, so it will happen again.
- She told me that they didn't care about the last project, so they won't care about this one either.
- That person always does that.
- I've taught with people like him before. He will act just like them.

Our brains are pattern-detectors and sometimes those patterns serve us well. But at other times, the frame that we use to perceive the situation gets in the way of us resolving a lingering difficulty in communication. And over time, it depletes an organization's ability to be able to use a strengths-based approach. (You'll recall that a core principle of a strengths-based approach is that we address challenges rather than bury them.) It may take a deliberate and intentional reframing of the situation to move us forward. Cognitive framing is a tool one can use as part of reflective thinking and investing in resilience (Pipas & Pepper, 2021). This technique is a conscious decision to identify and undo negative thinking patterns. In the context of schools, cognitive reframing can improve members' ability to resolve communication issues between educators and their students. Next, we'll lead you through a negative experience you've had at school and how to cognitively reframe it.

> *Cognitive framing is a tool one can use as part of reflective thinking and investing in resilience.*

NOTE TO SELF

Step 1 is to describe the situation. It helps to write things down so that you can clearly analyze the events as they occurred. Try to visualize the situation so that you can provide details.

1. DESCRIBE THE EVENT OR SITUATION.	
OUR EXAMPLE	YOUR EXPERIENCE
Tim is a member of your grade-level meetings. He often interrupts others with his own opinions about a topic and is regularly dismissive of other people's ideas. A regular refrain from him is "I've tried that before. It doesn't work."	

The second step is to identify your feelings. When this situation arises, what is or was your emotional response?

2. IDENTIFY YOUR EMOTIONS AND FEELINGS.	
OUR EXAMPLE	YOUR EXPERIENCE
I feel frustrated, angry, and resentful. I feel like my ideas are dismissed.	

Once you have identified your emotions, you'll want to examine your thoughts. Your thoughts might arise as you identify emotions, but you'll want to spend some time with these as it will help you reframe the situation. As you explore and explain your thoughts, consider what you believe the other person's intentions were. Ask yourself what you thought would happen or what might be the impact of these events. Consider the outcomes you expected.

3. EXPLORE AND EXPLAIN YOUR THOUGHTS.	
OUR EXAMPLE	YOUR EXPERIENCE
I think that Tim doesn't care about other people's efforts. It's disrespectful to me and I think it makes me look bad. I also think it's ruining my relationship with Tim.	

Once your thoughts have been explored and explained, you have the opportunity to reframe the situation or event. Consider if the intentions of the other person or people might be different from what you thought. Might there be other reasons for the behavior or actions? Could there be other outcomes or reasons that you could consider?

4. REFRAME THE EVENT OR SITUATION.	
OUR EXAMPLE	YOUR EXPERIENCE
Okay, maybe Tim is feeling ineffective. That might explain why he regularly says that something won't work. Or maybe he has an especially challenging class this year and it's bringing out his fears that he's not doing a good job.	

Once you have considered alternatives, you may want to test out your ideas and hypotheses. What if Tim is experiencing a really rough year, personally or professionally? Would that change how to feel about the situation? What if it is true that he's feeling ineffective because he has tried some things that haven't worked for him? What if there is no good reason for him dominating our discussions with such negativity—it's just a habit? Any of those situations

(Continued)

(Continued)

could be correct and it would be interesting to know. But, before you do your investigation and perhaps even make a change, consider your emotions following the reframing.

5. REVISIT YOUR FEELINGS.	
OUR EXAMPLE	YOUR EXPERIENCE
I need to have an honest conversation with Tim, with no one else present. But I actually feel a lot better thinking about this and realizing that it may not have anything to do with me. I want to find out about what he is experiencing. Maybe I could be of help to him. It's important that I have an honest and growth-producing conversation with him.	

CASE IN POINT

The leadership staff at Park High School are examining the results of the social capital survey they administered earlier in the month to learn about their own strengths as well as growth opportunities. It is important to note that the leadership team comprises administrators but also department chairs, a representation of classified staff, and the school's parent-teacher organization. As a school, they have been engaging in cultivating a strengths-based approach since last year and view social capital as one outcome of their efforts. Their quantitative analysis of their strengths and areas of growth is as follows:

STRENGTHS AT PHS	GROWTH OPPORTUNITIES AT PHS
• Teachers in this school have frequent contact with parents.	• Students respect others who get good grades.
• Parents of students in this school encourage good habits of schooling.	• Students in this school can be counted on to do their work.
• The learning environment here is orderly and serious.	• Community involvement facilitates learning here.

How would you advise the leadership team at the high school? Remember to keep a strengths-based approach in mind. You may want to revisit the opening section on what a strengths-based approach is and isn't, this time substituting the term *school* for *student* or *child*. In addition, you may have some thoughts on asset mapping.

MY RECOMMENDATIONS TO LEVERAGE STRENGTHS	MY RECOMMENDATIONS FOR GROWTH

Rath and Conchie (2009), authors of *Strengths-Based Leadership*, wrote that "if you focus on people's weaknesses, they lose confidence. At a very basic level, it is hard for us to build self-confidence when we are focused on our weaknesses instead of our strengths" (p. 14). Use the self-assessment tool that follows to reflect on your strengths as an educator.

Menu of Practices on a Strengths-Based Approach

Use the traffic light scale to reflect on your current practices as they relate to strengths at the levels of self, students, and school. What areas do you want to strengthen?

INDIVIDUAL OPPORTUNITIES	
I am aware of my strengths.	
I understand that my strengths can be cultivated.	
I can apply my strengths to enhance my resiliency.	
STUDENT-LEVEL OPPORTUNITIES	
I understand the connection between culturally sustaining pedagogies and the strengths of my students.	
I understand the importance of principles of self-determination in fostering student strengths.	
I use or plan to use a technique for learning about the assets my students bring to the class.	
I am intentional about my students' learning about their strengths.	
I use a strengths-based approach with students who are challenging to me.	
SCHOOL-LEVEL APPROACHES	
I am seeking to learn about the social capital at my school or district.	
My school uses strategies to build and foster social capital among students, staff, and families.	
I understand the links between a strengths-based approach and social capital.	
I actively engage in and take action to foster cognitive reframing for myself.	
I actively engage in and take action to foster cognitive reframing to assist colleagues facing a dilemma.	

● What do I need to do to change my reds to yellows?

● Who can support me to turn my yellows into greens?

● How am I using my greens to positively contribute to the good of the whole?

Access resources, tools, and guides for this module at
resources.corwin.com/theselplaybook

MODULE 2

....

IDENTITIES, BELONGING, AND PROSOCIAL SKILLS

wordclouds.com

BUILDING BACKGROUND

Belonging in school means that a person feels acceptance, respect, inclusion, and support. That goes for the adults and the students. In high-belonging schools, the learning environment honors who that person is and the various identities that comprise the individual. Notice that we said *identities*. There is a constellation of factors that make up our identities. Some of these are visible and others can be hidden. To understand identity, Satterfield (2017) suggests that we look at it through an iceberg activity. The majority of the iceberg is below the surface of the water, where we cannot see it. It's out of sight and yet we have to navigate around it, hoping we are not wrong.

> *There is a constellation of factors that make up our identities. Some of these are visible and others can be hidden.*

Dominique uses this identity exercise with students. They start off with voicing safe assumptions about him. They say he is male. Right; he identifies as male. They say he is tall. This is mostly right, as he stands at 6 feet. They say he's white. This is not true; he's mixed race. They say he is not married because he does not have a wedding ring; wrong. They say he is from Arizona and that his family is rich. Nope; he was born and raised in California, and his father was a construction worker and his mom worked in a residential facility for people with developmental disabilities until returning to school when Dominique was in high school. The students say that his name sounds like a girl's. Right, he explains, but he's named after a basketball player (Dominique Wilkins). They say he was into sports. Right. They say his first job was as a teacher. Wrong; he worked at Linens 'n Things before they went bankrupt.

What's the point of the iceberg activity? Personal experiences are deceiving, and people are much more complicated, complex, and interesting. We get a lot wrong when we simply look at a person and make assumptions. As Satterfield (2017) suggested, "Your job is to learn how to elicit each person's story and savor it." And he notes that it's important to know your own story and identity.

Elements of our identity include race, ethnicity, sex, gender identity, age, sexual orientation, physical attributes, personality, political affiliations, religious beliefs, professional identities, and more. Consider the visual in Figure 2.1, created by a Pennsylvania community training team. Of course, there are additional factors that could be included, such as trauma, political beliefs, and so on. The point is that people are complex and that there are many aspects of our identities.

Note that some of these identity factors are stable (e.g., height, skin color) and some develop over time (e.g., relationships, education). One of the most complex factors that influence identity formation is ethnicity, race, and culture. The ways members of a group define their group and how society defines these groups are continually evolving. Social identify theory (Figure 2.2) explores how a person's identity develops from their sense of who they are as part of the groups in which they belong. As Satterfield (2017) says, "we try to find our tribe while being able to connect with and to understand others."

There are several points worth noting in Figure 2.2. For example, there is an "in-group" and an "out-group," or *we* and *they*. This societal issue can be replicated in the classroom, making some students feel that they belong and others that they do not. A sense of belonging impacts educational success, motivation, attendance, and a host of other outcomes. As Bowen (2021) notes in a

FIGURE 2.1 IDENTITY WEB

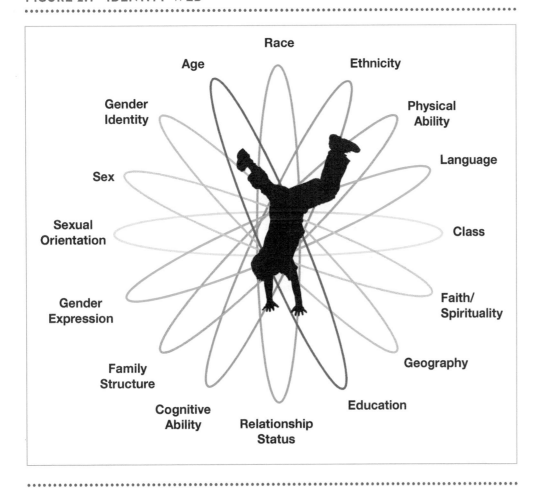

SOURCE: Allegheny County, Pennsylvania, DHS LGBTQ Community Training Team/SOGIE Project Team. Reprinted with permission. Image courtesy of iStock.com/sx70.

discussion with Gray, "Students choose to be in environments that make them feel a sense of fit."

Also, note that the in-group has a satisfied social identity, whereas the out-group has a dissatisfied social identity. When this occurs, social identity can become more important than one's individual identity.

> *"Students choose to be in environments that make them feel a sense of fit" (Bowen, 2021).*

School is a place in which individuals develop aspects of their identities. Given the number of hours that educators spend with students, there are powerful and life-changing experiences that we can facilitate to encourage positive individual and social identities or to thwart them. As an example, Jordan was asked to join a group for a project during the first week of school. Jordan's response: "Why? I'm just gonna fail. I'm the bad kid." When Jordan's teacher was able to have a private conversation, it became clear that Jordan had a history of failure, including multiple suspensions and disciplinary actions that Jordan had interpreted as identity. As Jordan said to the teacher, "Look, I'm not good at school, and you're just gonna kick me out like everyone else. So let's not pretend." Jordan's identity had already been shaped in significant ways by the social interactions that were experienced in his previous school.

FIGURE 2.2   SOCIAL IDENTITY THEORY

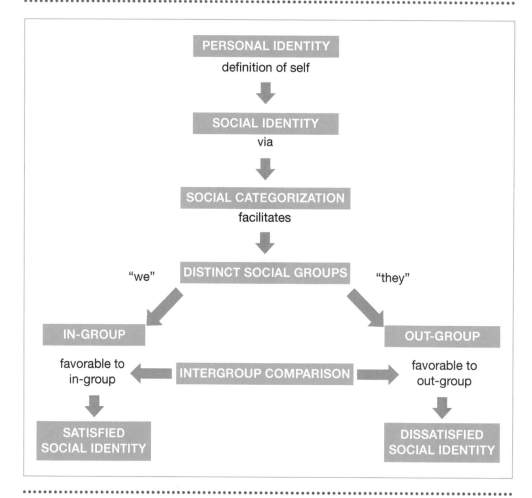

SOURCE: Y Studios (2020).

Of course, there are also positive interactions that educators have that shape student identities and their sense of belonging. Having high expectations with sophisticated support structures and letting students know that it is safe to be wrong are some of the things that we can do to ensure student success. As one teacher told her students, "When you get something wrong, it shows me you are being ambitious. Mistakes show me that you're taking a risk and not just playing it safe." In addition, the classroom and curriculum need to reflect the lived experiences of students and invite them into their culture and the cultures of others.

In this module, you will learn

- How your identity and belonging are shaped by your experiences

- About experiences that build a sense of belonging

- How to create a positive school identity

VOCABULARY SELF-AWARENESS

Directions: Consider the terms below.

- If it is new to you, write the date in the Level 1 column.

- If you have heard the word before but are not sure that you can use it in a sentence or define it, write the date in the Level 2 column.

- If this word is very familiar to you and you can define it and use it in a sentence, write the date in the Level 3 column.

Update your understanding of the terms as you engage in this module and in your work. Note that there are spaces for you to add terms that are new to you.

WORD	LEVEL 1	LEVEL 2	LEVEL 3	SENTENCE	DEFINITION
Identities					
Culture					
Belonging					
Identity-safe classrooms					
Prosocial skills					

(Continued)

(Continued)

WORD	LEVEL 1	LEVEL 2	LEVEL 3	SENTENCE	DEFINITION
Reputational capital					
Branding					

Level 1 = This word is new to me.

Level 2 = I have heard this word before.

Level 3 = I know the definition and I can use it in a sentence!

CASEL Connections for educators, students, and schools in this module:

SELF-AWARENESS	SELF-MANAGEMENT	SOCIAL AWARENESS	RELATIONSHIP SKILLS	RESPONSIBLE DECISION MAKING
Identities Assets		Identities Belonging Prosocial skills	Belonging Active listening Cultural competency	Reputational capital

IDENTITIES AND BELONGING BEGIN WITH SELF

Who am I?

That is certainly a question that has fueled philosophers, poets, scholars, and spiritual leaders across the span of human existence. The quest to understand oneself never ends, although how we define ourselves changes across experiences. Forging an identity as an educator begins with deepening your understanding of yourself. A common misconception is that being an educator requires that you are doing something to others: to students, to colleagues, to systems. And while taking action is crucial, it isn't effective if one's own identity is not understood. This first section of the module is designed to begin to explore your own identity in detail. Knowledge of one's own identity is a starting point for exploring self in relation to others.

> *Knowledge of one's own identity is a starting point for exploring self in relation to others.*

Self-knowledge is foundational to the work of social-emotional learning (SEL) in schools. The exploration of our own cultural influences and identities gives us insight into the frame we use to see the world and how that frame also limits our view. That's why cognitive reframing, discussed in the previous module, can be a useful tool. The interactions we have with others who have a different frame too often lead to misunderstandings between people. But our frame also informs how we perpetuate institutional and structural barriers that continue to do a disservice to children and communities. When others speak of dismantling systemic barriers, we must understand that we are a part of that system—we contribute to its maintenance. If we don't possess the knowledge of who we are and seek to cultivate a culture of belonging, how can we possibly expect others to do so?

WHAT'S *CULTURE*, ANYWAY?

Traditional definitions of *culture*, the ones we learned in school, usually focus on the explicit and implicit patterns of behavior, language, symbols, and values that make a human group distinct from others. We suppose that definition works in a historical sense when you're talking about a geographically isolated group of people who never intermingled with anyone else. But in a world connected by telecommunications and modes of travel, the idea that a person is a member of only one culture doesn't really fit. Think of all the possible cultural influences inside this person:

> A 32-year-old history teacher from Boston works in a rural school in Utah. He identifies as male, loves to listen to reggaeton music, and is learning Spanish on his own. His family is religious, although he doesn't practice the formal faith he was raised in. He is a first-generation American, and his family emigrated from India to escape oppression as a religious minority. He served in the American military as a special forces officer in Afghanistan. He creates fiber art on his own and has just joined a local art collective to display his work. He loves Mexican food and was thrilled to find a great restaurant nearby, where he and his boyfriend of four years eat weekly. He is out to the community but not to his parents, who keep hoping he'll meet a nice woman and get married.

Could you ever assign a single "culture" to this person? Our first cultural influences are derived from our families and expand over time as we have more experiences and interact with those outside of our family. Understanding our frame begins with looking at our own family experiences.

NOTE TO SELF

Begin your own cultural autobiography with a reflection about your family, either your family of origin or your family of choice.

When and where were you born?	
Where did you live between birth and age 18?	
Where did your parents grow up?	
Where did your grandparents grow up?	
What events did you celebrate as a family growing up?	
When there was a big decision to make in your family, who participated? Was there anyone who had the final word in major decisions?	
When you have a major decision to make as an adult, do you discuss it with your family, or do you only inform them once you have made a decision?	
As an adult, do you discuss your thoughts and feelings with your family?	
As an adult, do you discuss your thoughts and feelings with people outside of your family?	

RACIAL IDENTITY

Our cultural influences emanate from our family experiences but certainly do not end there. One's identity is further informed by race, sex, gender identity, sexuality, ethnicity, economic class, nationality, citizenship, religion, and ability.

We'll take one important identity, and that is race. Have you analyzed the experiences that have impacted your own racial identity? We have to confront the experiences we have had and analyze them for the messages that we have taken for granted. Doing so will open us to the possibilities that we have been shaped by society and that some of our beliefs are counter to the goals we have in becoming increasingly just. And coming to that understanding will allow us to take action and advocate for people who do not look like us. We all need to understand our racial autobiographies so that we can create safe places for our students and colleagues to learn (see Figure 2.3).

> *We all need to understand our racial autobiographies so that we can create safe places for our students and colleagues to learn (see Figure 2.3).*

It's hard to talk about, but all of us have been shaped by our ancestors. Doug vividly remembers a great uncle visiting San Diego from Alabama who refused to use a brand of soap because the TV commercial advertising it featured a Black man showering. This same great uncle's second wife told Doug to turn off Johnny Cash because she didn't like the sound of his *[retracted]* voice, but she used a derogatory term for skin color in her statement.

Dominique remembers his dad, who is Fijian, being stopped by the police in a suburban part of town where they live. The officer asked where he was visiting from and said that they didn't get a lot of Blacks in that part of town. Dominque's dad has driven very cautiously ever since and warns his children about their interactions with the police.

Each of these experiences and thousands more shape our views. Without analyzing them, and putting them to the equity test, we might end up thinking that other people are less or more deserving than us.

FIGURE 2.3 RACIAL AUTOBIOGRAPHY REFLECTIVE PROMPTS

Start with your **Racial Autobiography Bookends**. What can you recall about the earliest and most recent events and conversations about race, race relations, and/or racism that may have impacted your current perspectives and/or experiences?

- Earliest: What was your first personal experience in dealing with race or racism? Describe what happened.

- Most Recent: Describe your most recent personal experience in dealing with race or racism. Describe what happened.

To help you think about the time between your earliest and most recent racial experiences, jot down notes to answer the following questions. Let the questions guide but not limit your thinking. Note any other memories or ideas that seem relevant to you. When you have identified some of the landmarks on your racial

(Continued)

(Continued)

journey, start writing your autobiography. Remember that it is a fluid document, one that you will reflect on and update many times as your racial consciousness evolves.

1. **Family:**

   - Are your parents the same race? Same ethnic group? Are your brothers and sisters? What about your extended family—uncles, aunts, etc.?

   - Where did your parents grow up? What exposure did they have to racial groups other than their own? (Have you ever talked with them about this?)

   - What ideas did they grow up with regarding race relations? (Do you know? Have you ever talked with them about this? Why or why not?)

   - Do you think of yourself as white? As Black? As Asian? As Latinx? As Native American? Or just as "human"? Do you think of yourself as a member of an ethnic group? What is its importance to you?

2. **Neighborhood:**

   - What is the racial makeup of the neighborhood you grew up in?

   - What was your first awareness of race—that there are different "races" and that you are a member of a racial group?

   - What was your first encounter with another race? Describe the situation.

   - When and where did you first hear a racial slur?

   - What messages do you recall getting from your parents about race? From others when you were little?

3. **Elementary and Middle School:**

   - What was the racial makeup of your elementary school? Of its teachers?

   - Think about the curriculum: What Black Americans did you hear about? How did you celebrate Martin Luther King Jr. Day? What about Asian Americans, or Latinx individuals, or Native Americans?

   - Consider cultural influences: TV, advertisements, novels, music, movies, etc. What color God was presented to you? Angels? Santa Claus? The tooth fairy? Dolls?

   - What was the racial makeup of organizations you were in (Girl Scouts, soccer team, church, etc.)?

4. **High School and Community:**

   - What was the racial makeup of your high school? Of its teachers?

   - Was there interracial dating? Racial slurs? Any conflict with members of another race?

   - Have you ever felt or been stigmatized because of your race or ethnic group membership?

   - What else was important about your high school years, racially speaking— maybe something that didn't happen in high school but during that time?

- What is the racial makeup of your hometown? Of your metropolitan area? What about your experiences in summer camp, summer jobs, etc.?

5. **Present and Future:**

   - What is the racial makeup of the organization you currently work in? Of your circle(s) of friends? Does it meet your needs?

   - Realistically, think about where you want to live (if different from where you are now). What is its racial makeup? Social class makeup? Where do you want to work in the next 10 years? What is its racial makeup? Social class makeup?

6. **General:**

   - What's the most important image, encounter, whatever, you've had regarding race? Have you felt threatened? Have you ever felt in the minority? Have you felt privileged?

SOURCE: Courtesy of Glenn Singleton and Courageous Conversation™.

CASE IN POINT

Mike Alberts is a new colleague at a high school in a densely populated neighborhood in a large metropolitan area. He has more than 20 years of experience teaching advanced mathematical courses and self-identifies as white, middle-class, and "north of 50." He had previously taught in another nearby district in an affluent suburb. He was hired with strong letters of recommendation, advanced credentials, successful rounds of interviews, and a demonstration lesson. He noted in his interview that an area of weakness for him is that he hasn't had any experience in teaching in what he called "an urban school."

The mathematics instructional coach and the department chair will be working with Mr. Alberts to help him transition to the new school, as they are invested in making sure all members of the school community experience a strong sense of belonging. They were part of the hiring committee and recognized his talent as a math teacher, but also saw that he had some difficulty connecting with students. He is anxious, of course, to learn about his students. But when asked about his own cultural experiences, he dismisses them and says, "I don't have a culture. I'm white."

What advice do you have for the instructional coach and the department chair to support this teacher during his first year? Identify three experiences per quarter that would assist Mr. Albert.

(Continued)

(Continued)

1ST QUARTER EXPERIENCES	2ND QUARTER EXPERIENCES	3RD QUARTER EXPERIENCES	4TH QUARTER EXPERIENCES

IDENTITIES AND BELONGING CONTINUE WITH STUDENTS

Knowledge of the *identities* of students allows educators to create classrooms and schools that foster a sense of *belonging*. In order to discuss both, we will begin this section of the module with a further examination of belonging before moving into a powerful framework for defining a comprehensive approach to both.

INVEST IN YOUR STUDENTS' SENSE OF BELONGING

The research on belonging is extensive as it relates to a person's ability to achieve their aspirations. Maslow (1954) articulated this in his hierarchy of needs, noting that each level represents a need that must be met before advancing to the next level. Belonging is relevant to classrooms and schools as a prerequisite condition to self-esteem and achievement. In other words, when a young person's sense of belonging is compromised, their ability to achieve is endangered (see Figure 2.4).

FIGURE 2.4 MASLOW'S HIERARCHY OF NEEDS

SELF-ACTUALIZATION
Pursuing inner talent, creativity, fulfillment

SELF-ESTEEM
Achievement, mastery, respect, recognition

BELONGING AND LOVE
Friends, family, spouse, lover

SAFETY
Security, stability, freedom from fear

PHYSIOLOGICAL
Food, water, shelter, warmth

Our actions as educators communicate a sense of belonging (or not) to our students. Keyes (2019) conducted imaginative research with tenth-grade students. Although her intention was to uncover teacher actions that convey belonging, she did not share this with students. Instead, she asked them to identify and describe their favorite and least favorite ninth-grade class. Her findings were that two teacher actions built belonging:

1. Fostering relationships with and between students
2. Employing teaching practices that encouraged participation in the work for the class

These actions were expressed in a variety of ways that seem familiar:

FAVORITE CLASS		LEAST FAVORITE CLASS	
BUILDING RELATIONSHIPS	CONSTRUCTING A LEARNING ENVIRONMENT	BUILDING RELATIONSHIPS	CONSTRUCTING A LEARNING ENVIRONMENT
• The teacher shows all the students that they are respected and valued. • The teacher listens and incorporates students' ideas. • The teacher understands their developmental needs and incorporates them into the class.	• The teacher establishes clear, orderly, and consistent expectations and routines. • The teacher makes sure everyone understands and doesn't go forward until they do. • The teacher gives honest feedback. • The teacher offers opportunities to work with peers using clear directions.	• Students don't feel that the teacher likes them. • The teacher has difficulty relating to students. • The teacher provides inconsistent support with little follow-through.	• The teacher has favorite students. • The teacher frequently changes seats to punish students. • There is no class discussion or peer work. • The teacher lacked passion or interest in the course content.

Notice that these adolescents did not say that they needed the teacher to be their friend. What they did say is that in some classes they felt a stronger sense of belonging, while in other classes they did not. Further, they tied belonging to their teachers' actions. In other words, a sense of belonging is situational and is sensitive to the emotional environment. In the modules that follow, we will return to belonging through further discussion on curricular design to support belonging.

NOTE TO SELF

Caring educators cultivate a sense of belonging among their students. These practices are not left to chance and begin with the physical features of the classroom. Conduct an environmental scan of your classroom. Examine the following chart and note actions you take or help others take to create a sense of belonging. After you have finished, examine your reflection. What do you want to strengthen?

CHARACTERISTIC	HOW THIS IS EVIDENCED IN MY CLASSROOM
Students have a designated personal place for themselves and their possessions.	
Materials are accessible to students.	
Classroom agreements are posted, positively stated, and implemented.	
Student work is displayed.	
The classroom is clean and orderly.	
There is space for students to move around the classroom.	

INVEST IN IDENTITY-SAFE CLASSROOMS

Students and teachers bring with them a multitude of identities each day. A team of researchers, led by the late Dorothy Steele, have forwarded a framework they call *identity-safe* schools. Now led by Becki Cohn-Vargas, the research team leads work in making schools places where all students belong and learn. One hallmark of identity-safe classrooms is curriculum that reflects and promotes students' experiences using an assets-based approach. In addition, these classrooms reduce the level of stereotype threat that damages the learning of students. Their four-part framework, which aligns strongly with social-emotional learning, includes the following:

1. **Child-centered teaching,** promoting autonomy, cooperation, and student voice

   - *Listening for student voices* to ensure that each student can contribute to and shape classroom life

- *Teaching for understanding* so students will learn new knowledge and incorporate it into what they know

- *Focus on cooperation* rather than competition; each student learns from and helps others

- *Classroom autonomy* to promote responsibility and belonging in each student

2. **Cultivating diversity as a resource,** providing a challenging curriculum and high expectations for all students in the context of the regular and authentic use of diverse materials, ideas, and teaching activities

  - *Using diversity as a resource for teaching* to include all students' curiosity and knowledge in the classroom

  - *High expectations and academic rigor* to support all students in high-level learning

  - *Challenging curriculum* to motivate each student by providing meaningful, purposeful learning

3. **Classroom relationships,** based on trusting, positive interactions with the teacher and among the students

  - *Teacher warmth and availability to support learning* to build a trusting, encouraging relationship with each student

  - *Positive student relationships* to build interpersonal understanding and caring among students

4. **Caring classroom environments,** where social skills are taught and practiced to help students care for one another in an emotional and physically safe classroom

  - *Teacher skill* to establish an orderly, purposeful classroom that facilitates student learning

  - *Emotional and physical comfort* so each student feels safe and attached to school and to other students

  - *Attention to prosocial development* to teach students how to live with one another, solve problems, and show respect and caring for others (Identify Safe Classrooms, n.d.)

You'll find these themes throughout this playbook. However, for this module, we are going to build on listening, as evidenced in the first principle of child-centered teaching, as an important way teachers communicate their respect to young people. Now we invite you to further consider your listening experiences using a tool developed by the identity-safe classrooms research team (Cohn-Vargas et al., 2020).

How do you put listening to student voices into practice? Use this tool to reflect on your experiences. Then collect data from your own classroom to deepen your reflective thinking.

Reflect on your personal experience with speaking in a group, both when you were a student and in the present.

Do you feel free to speak up in groups?

What allows you to feel safe to speak up in one place but not another?

Consider your students who come from backgrounds different from yours.

How might their experience be like yours, and how might it be different?

Are any of your students' voices silenced, perhaps not by you, but by past experiences of being marginalized?

(Continued)

Observe the speaking patterns in your classroom. Make a simple tally of who is speaking in the group. Mark the initials of each child who speaks. We suggest you do this more than one time.

Analyze your data by asking yourself the following questions:

How many students in the class spoke out loud in the discussion?

Who spoke more than once?

Who did not speak at all?

What were the social identities of those who spoke and those who did not?

How can you extend opportunities to ensure everyone gets a chance to speak?

What kinds of encouragement can you give right in the moment as students speak?

SOURCE: Steele and Cohn-Vargas (2013).

PROMOTE THE PROSOCIAL SKILLS
NEEDED IN CARING CLASSROOMS

The social and emotional lives of students evolve throughout their educational careers. However, there are several overarching skills that deeply influence their relationships with teachers and peers. The Illinois State Board of Education was one of the first in the country to craft specific standards for SEL. They cast SEL as an issue of school wellness and identify five broad social skills needed for student success:

- Recognize and manage emotions

- Demonstrate caring and concern for others

- Establish positive relationships

- Make responsible decisions

- Handle challenging situations constructively

Many social-emotional curricula and programs have extensive materials and a scope and sequence of skills needed by students to promote positive peer relationships and a sense of belonging in the classroom and school. As well, they are attuned to the developmental needs of students. For instance, young children benefit from learning *prosocial skills* about sharing, while older students are developing the skills to resolve problems, come to a consensus, and make decisions. However, these efforts to teach students SEL are undermined when they are used as one-off lessons with little follow-through.

Feelings of belonging in the classroom are intertwined with the relative care peers demonstrate to one another. Kindness and compassion among students are crucial and are nurtured through daily investment. Teaching students to care for and about others is not going to be accomplished with isolated lessons on kindness. Rather, it needs to be infused into the dialogue and academics of the classroom and the school.

> Teaching students to care for and about others is not going to be accomplished with isolated lessons on kindness.

Kindness is a character strength and therefore is a malleable trait that can be fostered. The school and classroom climate play an important role in doing so. A recent study of nearly two thousand 13- to 17-year-olds found that there was a strong relationship between their perceptions of their own sense of belonging at school and their evaluation of school kindness, which is the level to which "students and others' needs are considered, and prosocial acts and positive relationships are encouraged" (Lee & Huang, 2021, p. 98). A culture of kindness exhibited through prosocial behaviors across the school contributes to a sense of belonging. As an example, some schools have specific student-driven actions for welcoming and connecting new students, such as peer-led orientations. Students who feel belonging in school are themselves kinder and have more positive relationships with peers and teachers (Patrick et al., 2007).

Prosocial behaviors are outward acts that are intentional acts that benefit others, Helping, sharing, volunteering, and comforting are all prosocial behaviors that are further associated with relatedness, which, you'll recall from Module 1, is not feeling alone (Eisenberg et al., 2015). And it turns out that prosocial behaviors are contagious. When these acts of kindness are witnessed by others, the observer, in turn, is more likely to behave in a prosocial manner (Dimant, 2019). Just as importantly, antisocial skills are even more contagious (Dimant, 2019). Classrooms and schools with a higher degree of antisocial behaviors are likely to spark similar actions among other students.

> Students who feel belonging in school are themselves kinder and have more positive relationships with peers and teachers.

Schoolwide prosocial efforts include activities that encourage volunteerism and service learning. Classroom efforts, especially those that are infused into the academic flow, reinforce for young people that we pull together to jointly solve problems. One of our favorite examples comes from a practice developed by a colleague, which she called Random Acts of Chemistry Kindness. She encouraged her students by assigning them to complete at least one act every quarter and to explain the chemistry involved. Some examples included a student who baked cookies for her classmates and explained what happened to the sugar when heated, and another who washed the desktops while discussing the role of detergents and surfactants.

Classroom processes can encourage or thwart prosocial behaviors. One seminal study is by Vivian Gussin Paley, a kindergarten teacher and researcher at the University of Chicago Lab Schools, who co-created a classroom norm with her students during a particularly rancorous year when she saw some of her students excluding others. "You can't say you can't play" became a rule as she and her students figured out together how peers would be included in activities. She wrote about her experiences in a book of the same title, noting, "We call it *play*. But it forms the primary culture in the classroom" (Paley, 1993, p. 29).

Classroom promises about how others are treated and spoken to, how students work together, and how care and concern are demonstrated can set a tone for expectations. Fourth-grade teacher Sarah Ortega co-constructs classroom promises with her students each year. One of the promises developed with her students for the 2021–2022 school year? "When you see someone who is sad, take their gray clouds away." And at the high school where the three of us work, we have three overarching rules:

- Take care of yourself.

- Take care of each other.

- Take care of this place.

Regardless of the grade span, intentional communication of prosocial values about sharing, helping, demonstrating concern for others, and working together should be a signature feature of classrooms and schools.

Examine the classroom and schoolwide practices at your site as they relate to prosocial skills. How are they encouraged? What new ideas do you have for enhancing them? Work with your colleagues to complete the following grid.

PROSOCIAL SKILL	YOUR CLASSROOM EFFORTS	YOUR SCHOOL EFFORTS	ADDITIONAL IDEAS TO STRENGTHEN
Helping			
Sharing			
Donating and volunteering			
Comforting			

CASE IN POINT

The faculty and administrators at Pine Tree Middle School have an experience that relatively few educators get to participate in: they will be opening the first new school in their district in more than 15 years. A core administrative staff was hired a few months earlier and most of the teaching faculty slots have been filled. As a part of the development of their school vision, the team had hosted numerous focus groups with community members, families of future students, as well as business and nonprofit leaders in their city. The emerging consensus was that a core mission of the school would be to foster belonging and the identities of its students.

Now the administrative team is preparing for a series of professional learning events with the teaching staff to move from vision to practice. An essential element of these efforts will center on students. Take what you have learned so far from these first two modules to advise the planners about considerations to keep in mind for building momentum.

CHARACTERISTICS	WHAT MIGHT THIS LOOK LIKE IN CLASSROOMS AT PINE TREE MIDDLE SCHOOL?
Building belonging through relationships	
Building belonging through learning environments	
Building identity through child-centered teaching practices	
Building student voice	

IDENTITIES AND BELONGING ARE NURTURED BY SCHOOLS

Much like individuals have identities, so do schools. These social organizations have histories that shape the identity of the school and the district or region they are part of. Sometimes, students are proud of their school. Other times, they are not. In some schools, students identify by the mascot, as in "We are Cardinals. Once a Cardinal, always a Cardinal." Other times, students say, "I go to a ghetto school" or "It's really not safe here. You gotta watch your back at this school."

SCHOOL IDENTITY AND REPUTATIONAL CAPITAL

Interestingly, the reputation of the school has an impact on students' overall learning. When students attend schools that they and their families believe are better, they actually perform better. As Willms (2013) noted, the different results of the Program for International Student Assessment (PISA) can be explained in part by the culture and climate of the school, as well as by the academic press and reputation of the school. The academic press and reputational capital become a self-fulfilling prophecy.

> The reputation of the school has an impact on students' overall learning.

So what is *reputational capital*? The business world defines it as the perception of the trust that customers and users have in your products, websites and services, and your brand. It comes down to one word: Trust. Do people trust your business? We will discuss relational trust (between people within the school) in an upcoming module, but trust in terms of reputational capital is about the reputation that the school has within the community. Building reputational capital requires being honest, delivering on the promises you make, and taking responsibility when you are wrong. Notice that there is a lot of individual responsibility required. Students, their families, and the community judge the school based on a sum of all the interactions they have with people associated with the school. In other words, what you say at the supermarket about the school can have an impact on the way people think about the school.

Of course, a single action can damage or destroy the reputation of a school. When a school or district is in the news for some awful thing that happened, some members of the community overgeneralize and assume that the entire school is a terrible place. That's when a public relations firm may be necessary to help tell other stories about the school. Remember, when schools have lower reputational capital, some of the students who should be attending the school exercise choice and transfer to different schools.

This brings us to another business term: *branding*. It's when we promote a product or company, usually using advertising and design. As *Entrepreneur* (n.d.) magazine noted, "Simply put, your brand is your promise to your customer. It tells them what they can expect from your products and services, and it differentiates your offering from that of your competitors."

Reread that definition and replace the word "customer" with "students and families," and "products and services" with "educational experience." That's school branding. In their book on school branding, Sinanis and Sanfelippo (2015) noted, "We want to ensure that OUR voices are the ones telling OUR story—we cannot let anyone else tell our story for us" (p. 7). They continue,

The idea of branding schools isn't about marketing kids or making false promises . . . it's about promoting the amazing things happening for those who don't have the opportunity to experience them on a daily basis. (p. 9)

What does this have to do with social-emotional learning, you may be asking? Well, the reputational capital of the school becomes part of the identity of the educators and students who work and learn in the organization. If you are interested in branding your school, take a look at Tracy Tigchelaar's (n.d.) "How to Create a Successful School Branding Strategy" blog post.

Given the ubiquity of social media, consider the messages that are sent by, and about, the school across various platforms. Some school staff members avoid social media because they recognize that it can encourage opinions and criticism. Others worry that their personal accounts will be targeted. However, there will be mentions about your school whether or not you choose to tell your story. Josh Meah & Company offers the following recommendations for using social media to create the reputational capital of the school:

- Complete your social media profiles using interesting photos and compelling copy. Include an attractive logo and cover image, contact info, and website address.

- Post regular and timely updates. Find out when most of your followers are online and post regularly at those times.

- Include captivating, high-quality images with posts to make them 650 percent more engaging than text-only updates.

- Add video to updates. Videos are the most popular type of content on Facebook and attract three times more shares than text-only posts.

- Use the 80/20 rule. Create 20 percent of the content you share and source 80 percent of it from other websites and blogs. Similarly, only 20 percent of your updates should be about the school, and 80 percent of them should pertain to subjects that parents and students are likely to find interesting. (Josh Meah & Company, 2019)

CASE IN POINT

The staff at Harbor Point Elementary School asked many members of the community, including parents of current students, the following questions:

- What three words would you use to describe our school?

- What feelings come to mind when you think about our school?

- What do you like best about our school?

- Would you recommend our school to your friends?

The data were startling but not surprising. The staff knew that the school did not enjoy a favorable reputation. Nearly 200 students who live in the neighborhood choose to attend different schools. The common terms used to describe the school were *depressing, nice teachers, no rigor, bad neighborhood,* and *prison.* The feelings included *fear, not welcome,* and *sad.* As one parent said, "My kid just isn't happy, and I worry that she's starting to hate school." Another said, "The teachers are nice, but I don't think that the students are learning very much." Over 60 percent of those surveyed said that they would not recommend the school but that the teachers were really nice to the students.

Obviously, the reputational capital of the school was not strong. However, the school had made progress over the past three years with increasing academic achievement. The quality of the instruction was strong with teachers supporting one another in implementation. And teacher morale was high. Together, they developed three goals:

1. Breakthrough academic results for students, combining rigor with support

2. Happy students and parents who loved their school

3. An improved sense of identity for teachers, students, and the school

Take each of these three goals and identify action steps the school could take to change the reputational capital of their school.

GOALS FOR HARBOR POINT ELEMENTARY	YOUR RECOMMENDATIONS
Goal 1: Breakthrough academic results for students, combining rigor with support	
Goal 2: Happy students and parents who loved their school	
Goal 3: An improved sense of identity for teachers, students, and the school	

SELF-ASSESSMENT

Emotionally and psychologically healthy young people are immersed in school environments that allow for them to learn about themselves and others. Use the self-assessment to determine the ways you contribute to this effort.

Menu of Practices on Identities and Belonging

Use the traffic light scale to reflect on your current practices as they relate to identities and belonging at the levels of self, students, and school. What areas do you want to strengthen?

INDIVIDUAL OPPORTUNITIES	
I have self-knowledge of my own cultural autobiography and its influence on me.	
I am exploring racial identity as a way to know more about myself.	
STUDENT-LEVEL OPPORTUNITIES	
I am able to use positive teacher relationships to build a sense of belonging for my students.	
I am able to construct a learning environment to build a sense of belonging with my students.	
I am able to incorporate elements of identity-safe classrooms as a way to build the social-emotional learning of my students.	
I regularly collect and analyze student participation data to improve identities and belonging for my students.	
I am intentional in fostering the prosocial skills of my students as it relates to helping, sharing, volunteering, and comforting.	
SCHOOL-LEVEL APPROACHES	
I am seeking to learn about the reputational capital at my school or district.	
I am knowledgeable about branding at my school or district.	
I have examined my school's or district's website with identities and belonging in mind.	

● What do I need to do to change my reds to yellows?

● Who can support me to turn my yellows into greens?

● How am I using my greens to positively contribute to the good of the whole?

Access resources, tools, and guides for this module at
resources.corwin.com/theselplaybook

MODULE 3

EMOTIONAL REGULATION

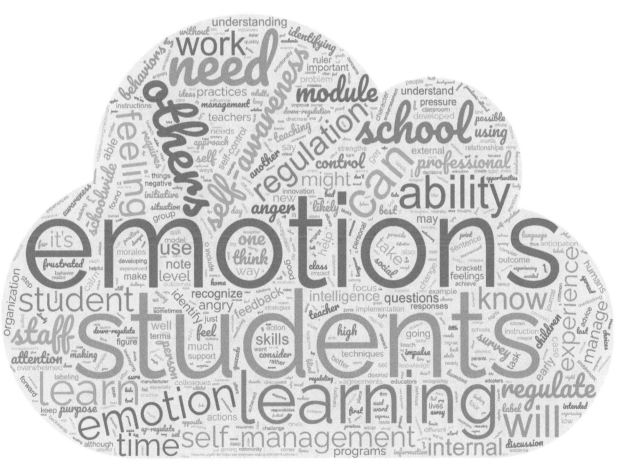

BUILDING BACKGROUND

It's nearing the end of a long day (week, month . . .), but not nearly close enough. The weather is cold and rainy, which made the commute home that much more difficult. You arrive home to two squabbling children who are in mid-argument about something, a stack of rain-soaked mail on the counter, and a dog who is looking at you because he needs to go out *now*. In the midst of all of this chaos, a text just came in from a colleague saying she has bad news and needs to talk to you *now*. The kids stop arguing just long enough to let you know that you need to settle their spat *now*.

How are you feeling?

In a previous module, we took a close look at character strengths and using a strengths-based approach when considering our own lives as well as those of our students and the school. In this module, we turn our attention to *emotional regulation*. The emotions we experience are more situational than character strengths. A way of thinking about them is that emotions govern our feelings, while character strengths can inform how we respond. That's a simple explanation of a complex relationship, but for the purposes of this playbook, it suffices.

> Emotions govern our feelings, while character strengths can inform how we respond.

In the best of circumstances, you can consciously identify what you're feeling on that rainy afternoon when you arrive home to chaos (*I'm frustrated, overwhelmed, spread too thin in this moment*). You find a way to reset yourself (*three deep breaths before I take all of this on*) and then formulate a rational response (*the older child is going to take the dog for a walk so I can separate them both, I'll talk to the other one, and I'll call my colleague back after I've restored some order here*). Or maybe you yell at both the kids and send them away while the dog cowers and slinks to another room at the sound of your angry voice. You experience a sense of shame and embarrassment in the now-empty kitchen, and you're still feeling overwhelmed and spread too thin.

It's fair to say that we've been on both sides, knowing at times we've been our best selves under duress, and other times not so much. Our ability to regulate our emotions, which is to say exerting some kind of influence over them, is a crucial way that humans change or suppress reactions so that they are more humane. Your emotional regulation helps you maintain relationships, manage distractions, and control impulsive behavior.

Up-Regulation and Down-Regulation

A pressure regulator is a control mechanism that manages the flow of a gas or a liquid. Let's use a common example of one—the pressure cooker you might have in your kitchen. Too much pressure internally is going to cause the lid to blow off. But if there's not enough pressure, you won't get the desired effect, which is cooking the food more quickly. The pressure regulator on the vessel is going to keep the pressure just right so that you can enjoy that delicious quinoa or chicken on time without having it explode all over the stove.

Your emotional regulator works similarly. In this case, it's referred to as up-regulation and down-regulation. We *up-regulate* when we turn up an emotion.

Many of the positive emotional management strategies you use are forms of up-regulation. For instance, we might concentrate on positive things that are happening, seek out positive people, or think of future events we are looking forward to (Livingstone & Srivastava, 2012). *Down-regulation* is just the opposite. There are times we turn down negative emotional responses to reduce the intensity of what we're feeling. We down-regulate to manage anxieties that are running ahead of our reasoning or to calm ourselves down when experiencing a level of anger that is outsize for the situation. Down-regulation of negative emotions can have a good effect on cardiovascular responses, such as heart and respiratory rates, as well as blood pressure (Zaehringer et al., 2020). As a link to Module 2, the ability to up-regulate and down-regulate contributes to emotional and physical well-being. Cognitive reframing is one technique that can support emotional regulation.

The ability to regulate emotions has implications for self, students, and how our schools work, especially in resolving problems.

The ability to regulate emotions has implications for self, students, and how our schools work, especially in resolving problems. In the module that follows, you will learn

- How emotional regulation and self-awareness are critical for how to understand ourselves and how we interact with others

- About labeling emotions and teaching self-management and self-control

- How to identify innovation and implementation of schoolwide initiatives regarding emotional regulation

VOCABULARY SELF-AWARENESS

Directions: Consider the terms below.

- If it is new to you, write the date in the Level 1 column.
- If you have heard the word before but are not sure that you can use it in a sentence or define it, write the date in the Level 2 column.
- If this word is very familiar to you and you can define it and use it in a sentence, write the date in the Level 3 column.

Update your understanding of the terms as you engage in this module and in your work. Note that there are spaces for you to add terms that are new to you.

WORD	LEVEL 1	LEVEL 2	LEVEL 3	SENTENCE	DEFINITION
Emotional regulation					
Up-regulation					
Down-regulation					
Emotional intelligence					
Self-awareness					
Self-management					

WORD	LEVEL 1	LEVEL 2	LEVEL 3	SENTENCE	DEFINITION
Identifying emotions					
Self-control					
Diffusion of innovation					

Level 1 = This word is new to me.

Level 2 = I have heard this word before.

Level 3 = I know the definition and I can use it in a sentence!

CASEL Connections for educators, students, and schools in this module:

SELF-AWARENESS	SELF-MANAGEMENT	SOCIAL AWARENESS	RELATIONSHIP SKILLS	RESPONSIBLE DECISION MAKING
Identifying emotions	Emotional regulation Up-regulation Down-regulation Self-control	Emotional intelligence Recognition of others' emotions		Diffusion of innovation

EMOTIONAL REGULATION BEGINS WITH SELF

Salovey and Mayer's (1990) groundbreaking work in *emotional intelligence* (EI) has illuminated the importance of emotional recognition and regulation in the lives of adults. In terms of our professional lives as educators, it exerts an influence on our

- Grading practices (Brackett et al., 2013)
- Discipline practices (Valente et al., 2019)
- Ability to recognize SEL development in students (Walton & Hibbard, 2019)

This last point is of particular interest, as the researchers found that a teacher's EI had an outsized influence, beyond professional training, in their ability to recognize their students' competence.

Emotional intelligence is defined through a four-branch model developed by Mayer and Salovey (1997) as the ability to

- Perceive accurately, appraise, and express emotion
- Access and/or generate feelings when they facilitate thought
- Understand emotion and emotional knowledge
- Regulate emotions to promote emotional and intellectual growth (p. 10)

Think of these as branches on a tree, with the lower limbs needed to access the higher ones. The first and second are accurately appraising your emotional state or that of another person, which then can allow you to consider the emotion being experienced and think about it. The ability to do so allows you to climb up to a higher branch, which is having the emotional knowledge to understand that some emotions intersect with others and may amplify what is being experienced (think of the frazzled parent in the opening scenario). The highest branch of that emotional intelligence tree is being able to regulate one's emotions.

INVEST IN YOUR EMOTIONAL INTELLIGENCE

Self-awareness is key to developing your emotional intelligence. Unfortunately, it seems like nearly all of us have a blind spot when it comes to our awareness of our emotional intelligence. Eurich (2018), an organizational psychologist, noted in *The Harvard Business Review* that 95 percent of respondents to a survey reported that they had high levels of self-awareness, although their analysis reported that only 10 to 15 percent of them actually met those levels. She goes on to explain that self-awareness is both outward- and inward-facing. There's internal self-awareness, which is how well you know yourself, and external awareness, which is how well you understand how you are perceived by others. Both are important, and both are enhanced by seeking feedback from others.

Let's start with internal self-awareness. This is a measure of one's ability to notice and understand one's emotions, character strengths, and behaviors. This is a crucial skill for emotional regulation. However, it must be balanced by external self-awareness to better understand how your emotions, character strengths, and behaviors are being projected. A person who is highly self-aware internally but has a limited view of how they are understood by others may be, in Eurich's language, an "introspector" who doesn't seek to uncover blind spots.

Conversely, a person highly oriented to how they are looked on by others but who spends little time cultivating an internal awareness is described as a "pleaser" who might make choices that are not in their own best interests (see Figure 3.1).

FIGURE 3.1 FOUR SELF-AWARENESS ARCHETYPES

	LOW EXTERNAL SELF-AWARENESS	HIGH EXTERNAL SELF-AWARENESS
HIGH INTERNAL SELF-AWARENESS	**Introspectors** They're clear on who they are but don't challenge their own view or search for blind spots by getting feedback from others. This can harm their relationships and limit their success.	**Aware** They know who they are and what they want to accomplish, and they seek out and value others' opinions. This is where leaders begin to fully realize the true benefits of self-awareness.
LOW INTERNAL SELF-AWARENESS	**Seekers** They don't yet know who they are, what they stand for, or how their teams see them. As a result, they might feel stuck or frustrated with their performance and relationships.	**Pleasers** They can be so focused on appearing a certain way to others that they could be overlooking what matters to them. Over time, they tend to make choices that aren't in service of their own success and fulfillment.

SOURCE: Eurich (2018).

INVEST IN EMOTIONAL REGULATION WITH OTHERS

Emotional regulation isn't an entirely internal process; it is the fuel that makes personal and professional relationships work. While we experience emotions internally, their expression impacts others. As discussed in the previous section, external self-awareness is equally important. The disposition to seek feedback from others can serve you well in understanding how you are perceived.

> *The disposition to seek feedback from others can serve you well in understanding how you are perceived.*

This concept is sometimes overlooked in the Visible Learning research, and it speaks to a misconception about the nature of teaching and learning. Some are tempted to focus on the more overt teaching strategies in that research, such as jigsaw or reciprocal teaching, while overlooking another essential disposition, which lies in understanding that student learning is feedback to oneself as an educator. Some examples include feedback from students to improve instruction (0.53), microteaching to understand the impact of one's instruction (0.88), and most of all, teacher estimates of student achievement (1.46). This last one speaks to the very nature of teaching and learning as a dynamic and responsive exchange between students and teachers and is informed by assessment data that are used to set the next challenge. These informed judgments are drawn from monitoring a student's progress and leveraging it to accelerate learning.

> *Student learning is feedback to oneself as an educator.*

Seeking and utilizing feedback is also essential for teams to work. Another strong influence on student learning is collective teacher efficacy (CTE). This is the shared belief by a group of teachers in a particular educational environment that they have the skills to positively impact student outcomes. At 1.36, it has the potential to significantly accelerate student achievement (visiblelearningmetax.com). Building a team's CTE requires close monitoring of student learning, especially in identifying who is learning and who is not, and then responding to the challenge. In the context of this module, it also requires that team members are able to seek and utilize feedback while maintaining the social fabric of the group (Fisher et al., 2020).

Far too often, however, we make assumptions that somehow the adults will get to know each other and figure out how to navigate the complexities of working shoulder-to-shoulder with others. In the next Note to Self we're going to ask you to put your internal self-awareness to work by crafting information about yourself for your colleagues to use. This can spark some important dialogue as you get feedback about yourself while doing so in a way that is meant to be fun.

NOTE TO SELF

Think of the last appliance you bought. Chances are very good that it came with a user's manual that noted its features, provided information about its limitations, and included some safety reminders so you wouldn't damage the machine or hurt yourself. If you created a user's manual for yourself, what might it say? Nancy developed one for herself as an example, inspired by Chris Balchut's (2021) personal user's manual. What might yours say?

The Basics: Nancy	**The Basics:**
Manufacture: 1959 in Long Beach, CA	**Manufacture:**
Model: Female (she, her, hers)	**Model:**
Languages: English	**Languages:**
Primary Uses: generating ideas, locating resources, listening	**Primary Uses:**

Preferred Environments	**Preferred Environments**
Home, medium-energy settings, small team meetings	
Topics of Conversation	**Topics of Conversation**
Literacy, best practices in education, her family, Pittsburgh Steelers football	
Warnings and Manufacturer Defects	**Warnings and Manufacturer Defects**
Feels anxious often Gets overwhelmed when there are too many things happening all at once	
Do Not Push These Buttons	**Do Not Push These Buttons**
Giving up on students Limiting student experiences based on disability	
Avoid Personal Injury	**Avoid Personal Injury**
If Nancy doesn't get back to you right away, it's not because she doesn't care; time management is a bit of a struggle	
Operating Instructions	**Operating Instructions**
Best hours are 7:00 AM–6:00 PM Shuts down by 8:30 PM Best way to contact is by email or text	
Environment	**Environment**
Quieter settings are better so she can hear herself think Operates best in smaller groups	
Care and Maintenance	**Care and Maintenance**
Reciprocate: Set goals together so you can work toward a common outcome *Avoid overhandling:* Nancy will likely shut down if you ask her to do too many things at the same time *Feedback:* She welcomes feedback that is humane and growth producing	
Assistance	**Assistance**
Ask Doug, Ian, or Dominique for advice if she is not performing as you expected	

CASE IN POINT

Sara Quezado was appointed as a new vice principal at Redwood Hills High School. With a student population of nearly 2,500 and 153 classified and certificated staff members, Ms. Quezado has a lot of people to get to know. There's also the excitement (and stress) of stepping into a new role. This is a career advancement for the first-time administrator, one she has been seeking, but it also comes with some anxiety. Some of it is personal, including balancing home responsibilities and the needs of her aging parents. Other concerns come from the execution of her new professional responsibilities. She had previously been a science instructional coach at another high school and had served as an induction support provider for new science teachers in the district. But this will be different—a much larger staff, a leadership team she is just getting to know, and lots of students and families.

Ms. Quezado is cognizant that emotional regulation and self-awareness are an integral part of her ability to perform at the high standards she has set for herself, personally and professionally. Using what you have learned so far in this playbook, how might you advise her? Keep in mind that she is in a new role, so simply having her do what she has always done in the past might not be sufficient.

Life-work balance	
Maintaining physical and emotional well-being	

Leveraging character strengths	
Regulating her own emotions	
Developing her internal self-awareness	
Developing her external self-awareness	

EMOTIONAL REGULATION CONTINUES WITH STUDENTS

Much of what we discussed in the previous section, which was focused on your own emotional regulation, applies to students too. Like adults, students make mistakes with their emotional regulation and under-react or overreact. They are still developing the skills to recognize and manage their emotions. And we all know that when someone is in a high emotion state, learning is compromised. Jones et al. (2017) note that "children must learn to recognize, express, and regulate their emotions before they can be expected to interact with others who are engaged in the same set of processes" (p. 16). The whole point of having emotions is to focus our attention and motivate us to take action. Think of a feeling that you've recently experienced. What is that feeling telling you to focus on? We need to discard the idea that some emotions are good and others are bad. We are emotional beings, and our emotions help us make decisions and take action. It's when we fail to regulate our actions that bad things can happen. But the emotion itself is not bad (or good).

> *Emotion itself is not bad (or good).*

Emotional regulation for students begins with learning the names of emotions and matching those labels to the feelings that are going on inside. For younger students, the zones of regulation (Kuypers, 2013) provide a color-based vocabulary for expressing emotional states:

- **Blue zone:** I am feeling sad, sick, tired, bored, moving slowly
- **Green zone:** I am feeling happy, calm, okay, focused, ready to learn
- **Yellow zone:** I am feeling frustrated, worried, silly/wiggly, excited, a little out of control
- **Red zone:** I am feeling mad/angry, terrified, yelling/hitting, elated, out of control

Using this system, students learn that

- We all have emotions.
- There are names for the feelings that we have.
- Emotions are not good or bad.
- There are ways to respond when you experience a specific emotion.

Older students are introduced to a more complex model of emotions, such as the framework developed by Plutchik (2002; see Figure 3.2), which suggests that there are eight basic emotions: joy, trust, fear, surprise, sadness, anticipation, anger, and disgust. Notice that this model creates opposites:

- Joy is the opposite of sadness.
- Fear is the opposite of anger.
- Anticipation is the opposite of surprise.
- Disgust is the opposite of trust.

This model also acknowledges combinations, such as how anticipation and joy combine to become optimism, and joy and trust combine to become love. Plutchik (2001) believed that humans have the capacity to experience 34,000 unique emotions. Emotions are complex and being able to recognize that there may be many emotions occurring simultaneously is a valuable skill, especially when it comes to regulating those emotions.

FIGURE 3.2 WHEEL OF EMOTIONS

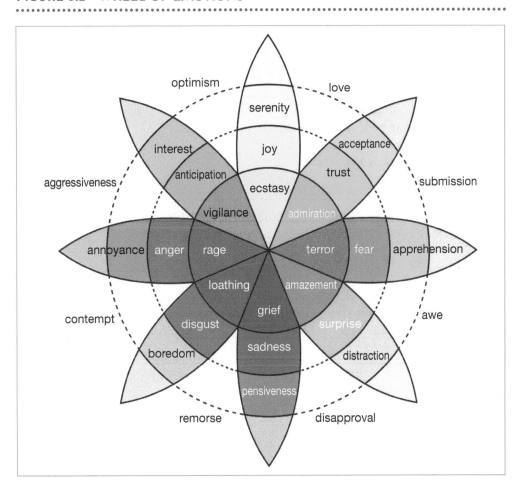

SOURCE: Emotional Wheel by Robert Plutchik.

The group Six Seconds (n.d.) provides a free download of their Emotoscope (www.6seconds.org/free-emotoscope-feeling-chart), which organizes emotions into categories and then provides a list of words, a sentence, the purpose, and the sensation for each emotion. The document is four pages long and can be used to teach students about their emotions. For example, in the category *mad*, *annoyed* is one of the words.

- The *sentence* reads: I feel annoyed because things are not going my way.

- The *purpose* reads: Focus attention on a problem you've ignored. Note that each emotion serves a purpose for the person experiencing it.

- The *sensations* are agitation, headache, tense muscles.

As another example, in the category *glad*, *confident* is one of the words.

- The *sentence* reads: I feel confident because I know I can meet my goals.
- The *purpose* reads: Reinforce the value of your efforts.
- And the *sensations* are eyes relaxed, head held high, relaxed body.

One of the benefits of this Emotoscope is the sensation experienced as these words help students identify what they are feeling and then create a label for the experience.

Brackett and Frank (2017) suggest that students be provided with regular opportunities to gauge their emotional state in different settings. They provide four questions that educators can use to invite self-reflection and discussion:

1. How do you feel at the start of the school day?

2. What emotions do you feel throughout the day while learning?

3. Do you feel differently when walking in the hallway, sitting in the lunchroom, or at recess or passing period?

4. How do you feel at the end of the school day?

These questions require that students recognize their feelings and have names for them. This is the first step to regulating emotions and developing habits that are appropriate responses to the range of emotions we all experience throughout our day.

NOTE TO SELF

Consider the ways in which you can teach students about emotions, specifically how to name the emotions that they experience. Some ideas are included below that you might adapt or adopt. These are all from our colleagues who offered some ideas. They may or may not all work for you. Take note of ideas you have for this aspect of teaching.

ADVICE FROM A COLLEAGUE	MY ADOPTION OR ADAPTATION PLAN
Create a place in the classroom where emotions are posted and have students identify which emotions they are experiencing.	

ADVICE FROM A COLLEAGUE	MY ADOPTION OR ADAPTATION PLAN
Notice the emotions of characters in books as you are reading. Label the emotions and talk about the way that you knew that the character was experiencing that emotion.	
Host class check-ins using the questions from Brackett and Frank (2017) inviting students to describe what they are feeling.	
Provide each student with an emotion wheel to keep at their desk so that they can refer to it when their state changes.	
Play emotional charades. Have students write down emotions on slips of paper and draw one at a time with a volunteer student acting it out while the class attempts to name it.	
Create writing prompts and journal entries in which students describe a situation and their emotional response.	

Additional ideas from colleagues:

Recommendations for my colleagues:

SELF-MANAGEMENT AND SELF-CONTROL

Recognizing emotions is one side of the equation. The other side is the ability to manage the response to those emotions. As we noted in the opening scenario, there are more and less effective responses to our emotions. But remember, our emotions are designed to focus attention and motivate us to action. The problem is, some of the actions humans take hurt themselves or others. Thus, part of the social-emotional learning (SEL) that students need relates to *self-management* and *self-control*, or "the ability to regulate one's emotions, thoughts, and behaviors effectively in different situations" (Transforming Education, 2020). Importantly, academic learning is impacted by the learner's ability to alter or override problematic actions and regulate behavior, thoughts, and emotions. The effect size of self-control is 0.49, above average in terms of the impact on learning (visiblelearningmetax.com).

> *Academic learning is impacted by the learner's ability to alter or override problematic actions and regulate behavior, thoughts, and emotions.*

As students learn self-management and self-control, they will probably make mistakes. We need to be careful with the punishments we dole out, as students are learning to manage their actions and reactions. That does not mean that consequences are avoided, but rather that public humiliation, shame, and exclusionary practices such as suspension and expulsion should be avoided.

We can't imagine a student who learned to regulate emotions and develop self-management skills from a clip chart that publicly displays the fact that there will be a call home to parents, or from a suspension for making a bad choice. Again, consequences can be used to shape behavior, but exclusion and shame do very little else besides create anger. For alternatives to these control-and-exclude techniques, see Smith et al. (2022).

As part of self-management, students must learn to control their anger. It starts by recognizing that anger is a secondary emotion. Before we feel angry, we experience another emotion, such as sadness, jealousy, surprise, or embarrassment. When a student becomes angry, if they can identify the primary emotion, they are much more likely to be able to regulate their actions. Thus, it is important to teach students about anger and how it comes after another emotion.

There are also techniques for anger management that can be learned. The Mayo Clinic (2020) offers 10 tips that can be taught to students:

1. **Think before you speak.** Before saying something that you regret, take some time to think about what you want to say. Students need to learn to push "pause" when they are angry and think about what they want to say. It may be useful to have a countdown from 10 to 1 before saying something.

2. **When calm, express your anger.** When you have had time to think, share what made you angry and why it did. Share your concerns or needs without hurting others. Students must learn that anger is one of many emotions that humans experience and that there are ways to resolve that feeling.

3. **Get some exercise.** Movement can help reduce the stress caused by becoming angry. Invite students to walk it off or do some other enjoyable movement-related task. If they learn to recognize when they are angry and

why, and then take some time to move, the next course of action will likely be more positive.

4. **Take a self-initiated timeout.** We all need breaks. Creating opportunities for students to remove themselves from situations that cause anger and re-group is helpful and can aid students in calming down and making appropriate choices.

5. **Identify possible solutions.** Rather than focusing on what made you mad, figure out what the solution is. Understanding the underlying emotion is critical to identifying solutions. And sometimes, we have to realize that there is little we can do about a situation and that we need to rethink our reaction to it.

6. **Stick with "I" statements.** Using I-statements is helpful in shaping the responses of others. When we feel blame and shame from others, we are likely to become defensive and then angry. When students learn to use I-statements to describe the problem and what they need, the listeners are more likely to be able to listen and take action.

7. **Don't hold a grudge.** Forgiveness is powerful and allows for friendships to be repaired or for people to co-exist. When we learn to make amends and forgive, we learn from the situation and are less likely to engage in the same problematic actions in the future.

8. **Use humor to reduce tension.** When students learn to use humor to reduce their anger, their actions will likely be more positive. We are not suggesting that we simply make light of a situation or use sarcasm, but rather that it can help to learn to use humor to figure out what is making you angry. Humor can also help with some of the unrealistic expectations we have for ourselves and others.

9. **Practice relaxation and calming techniques.** Actions such as deep breathing, imagining a relaxing place, massaging temples, repeating a calming phrase, listening to music, writing in a journal, doing a yoga pose, are all options that students might choose to calm themselves down when they are angry.

10. **Know when to get help.** Asking for help is a sign of strength. Sometimes, students are in a situation that has made them angry and they are not sure what to do. If they recognize that they cannot control their anger, it's important that they learn to ask for help. This may be from peers or adults, but learning that it's okay to ask for help is a significant step in learning self-control.

There are other aspects of self-management that students need to learn, such as impulse control. The evidence on teaching impulse control suggests that students learn to label their feelings and develop anger management skills (e.g., Morin, 2021). In addition, and perhaps more specifically, teaching impulse control requires recognizing what is causing the impulsivity. For example, if the student does not listen to directions and instead forges forward, it's helpful to have them repeat the directions or tell the directions to another person. Of course, the directions need to be age appropriate in terms of the number of steps and the complexity of those steps.

Teaching impulse control requires recognizing what is causing the impulsivity.

In addition, it's useful to teach problem-solving skills. Students have to learn that there is more than one way to solve a problem, be that mathematics or a conflict with a peer. Students need practice with brainstorming possible solutions and then evaluating which solution is likely to be most effective. And this practice needs to include academic as well as social-emotional learning.

Further, when there are consistent expectations in the classroom, impulse control becomes less of a problem. When constructed with the class and used to provide feedback, classroom agreements are useful for helping students with impulse control. For example, consider the following classroom agreements developed by a group of fourth graders and their teacher:

1. Everyone is different, and that makes us special.
2. We will not judge anyone by their size, skin color, dreams, sexual orientation, or gender.
3. Making mistakes is proof that we are trying.
4. When you see someone feeling sad, take away their gray clouds.
5. Being in the Learning Pit [see Module 5] is natural. We do the work to get out.
6. We work hard to achieve our dreams.

They did not say "don't hit the person next to you" or "raise your hand before speaking." These are givens and the way that the class operates. Instead, the class developed agreements that would guide the ways in which they interacted with others. As their teacher said, "This really helps with the impulse control as we work on these agreements every day. The students are getting much better at thinking about these agreements before they take action."

NOTE TO SELF

Self-management skills include anger management and impulse control, as well as a list of other areas of personal responsibility. We have outlined several additional skills that students need to develop. Read through these skills and identify opportunities to teach this skill in your classroom.

SKILL	DEFINITION	IDEAS FOR TEACHING
Organization	The ability to plan, prioritize, complete important tasks and activities, and keep your space and belongings in order	

SKILL	DEFINITION	IDEAS FOR TEACHING
Goal setting	The ability to identify what you want to accomplish in a clear way; these goals are achievable and specific	
Time management	The ability to prioritize important tasks and maintain a focus on completing those tasks; it includes the ability to establish deadlines and monitor the completion of your responsibilities	
Self-motivation	The ability to take initiative and the desire to succeed; rather than relying on external forces, there is an internal recognition of a task well done	
Stress management	The ability to manage pressure, deadlines, and thoughts that might detract from the successful completion of tasks and assignments	
Delaying gratification	The ability to control impulses and delay satisfaction or the reward for completing a task or activity	

CASE IN POINT

Sixth-grade teacher Javier Morales has a group of students who "act out." These students, spread across the periods of his day, are typically off task and disruptive. Sometimes they shout out in class, and other times, some of them seem withdrawn. It does not take much to push their buttons, and they react quickly and often in anger. Individually, each of these students is likable, has friends, and tries hard in their classes. When Mr. Morales meets with them individually, they each have hopes for their future and tell him that he is a good teacher.

Mr. Morales is getting frustrated with the situation, concerned that they are not learning all that they could. He is especially concerned about their social and emotional development, given that seventh and eighth grade will be an increased academic challenge for them. As he devotes time to his students' emotional regulation, Mr. Morales notes that they only know the names of basic emotions (e.g., happy, sad) and that they have few techniques for regulating their emotions. What advice would you give to Mr. Morales?

First step	
Which labels for emotions should they learn immediately?	
Which area of emotional regulation should be initiated first?	
How will Mr. Morales know he is successful?	
How might Mr. Morales involve his students (those that are acting out and those who are not) in the solution?	

EMOTIONAL REGULATION IS NURTURED BY SCHOOLS

Emotional regulation is a component of nearly every social-emotional learning initiative. Although these programs vary somewhat in terms of specific language and techniques, they all work best when applied as a schoolwide approach. The value in adopting practices that are utilized throughout the school is that it creates an environment that facilitates emotional regulation beyond individual classrooms. There are many excellent programs that exist and some variance in how this element is referred to in programs, including *self-management*, *emotion management*, and *self-awareness*. However, critical elements of emotional regulation appear across programs for elementary and secondary students. The Collaborative for Academic, Social, and Emotional Learning (CASEL, n.d.a) offers an online comparison tool of well-known programs at pg.casel.org.

> *Social-emotional learning initiatives work best when applied as a schoolwide approach.*

THE NEED FOR A SCHOOLWIDE APPROACH

A survey of 22,000 high school students conducted by the Yale Center for Emotional Intelligence found that students experienced negative emotions 75 percent of the time when they were in school, prompting Brackett, director of the Center and lead developer of RULER, an evidence-based approach to SEL, to wonder, "What does this mean for teaching and learning? . . . How much attention are they paying to their schoolwork?" (Brackett, quoted in Heller, 2017, p. 21).

The need for a schoolwide effort is clear. The need to learn how to emotionally regulate is not something that only *some* students need. Emotions are an integral part of learning. Negative emotions thwart learning (recall the negative influences discussed in Module 1, including anxiety and boredom). One small study, published in the prestigious journal *Mind, Brain, and Education*, used a measure of emotional intelligence with 9- and 10-year-old participants. They found that the children showed a marked decline in intrapersonal, interpersonal, and adaptability scales as a result of pandemic-altered schooling. Further, they called for intentional efforts to increase the emotional intelligence of young people through schoolwide initiatives (Martín & Santiago, 2021).

RULER, an acronym that stands for Recognizing, Understanding, Labeling, Expressing, and Regulating, is one of several CASEL Select evidence-based approaches to SEL. We chose to profile RULER because it is offered for pre-kindergarten through high school students. The focus is on operationalizing the abstract concepts that comprise social-emotional learning by equipping schools, and the adults and young people in them, with concrete tools to enact what they call "RULER skills" (Brackett et al., 2019, p. 145):

- **Recognize** our own emotions and those of others, not just in the things we think, feel, and say but in facial expressions, body language, vocal tones, and other nonverbal signals

- **Understand** those feelings and determine what experiences actually caused them

- **Label** our emotions with a nuanced vocabulary

- **Express** our feelings in accordance with cultural norms and social contexts

- **Regulate** our emotions by using helpful strategies for dealing with what we feel and why

One tool promoted by RULER is the Mood Meter Check-In, a core routine that students and teachers can use regularly. This is an app that allows an entire class to plot where they are emotionally so that the teacher can take the group's emotional temperature. Similar to the zones of regulation discussed in the previous section, the Mood Meter is based on colors that plot across an x-axis (pleasant to unpleasant) and a y-axis representing energy (high energy to low energy). Each quadrant contains 25 emotion words to assist students in labeling their emotions. What's most important, of course, is what you do with it. Because RULER is designed to be embedded within the academic program, rather than siloed as separate content, it provides teachers with techniques for integrating emotional regulation into the class.

The school-facing side of RULER notes the importance of implementation as more than a simplistic "one-size-fits-all" approach for the adults. They use a *diffusion of innovation* approach to implementation developed by Rogers (1962/2003) to understand how an initiative spreads (diffuses) over time. RULER challenges schools to identify and differentially support

- **Innovators** who bring the initiative forward, lead, and continue to innovate through the duration

- **Early adopters** who are eager to pilot (about 15 percent of the staff)

- **Early majority users** who represent the first significant wave of users after witnessing successes and challenges of the early adopters (roughly one-third of the staff)

- **Late majority users** who come on board due to the momentum created in the organization (another one-third of the staff)

- **Laggards** who are slower to change and adapt and may need more support (about 15 percent of the staff)

A school that has a higher degree of social capital is likely to diffuse an innovation more quickly because of the network of relationships present.

The knowledge that initiatives of any kind are far more complex than a top-down decree might suggest prepares an organization better for the implementation dips and detours that are going to occur. Diffusion of innovation rests squarely on the social capital of an organization to adopt an initiative slowly or more quickly. A school that has a higher degree of social capital is likely to diffuse an innovation more quickly because of the network of relationships present among staff, students, and families. As well, a staff that possesses a higher degree of emotional regulation is going to be better equipped to resolve problems, discuss ideas, and work through other challenges.

Imagine that you are advising a school about an initiative they are considering related to emotional regulation. What kinds of specialized supports would you recommend for each of these groups? Use your own emotional intelligence to consider what their view might be.

ADOPTERS	WHAT EMOTIONS MIGHT THEY BE FEELING?	WHAT SUPPORTS DO THEY NEED?
Innovators ≈ 2.5%		
Early adopters ≈ 13.5%		
Early majority ≈ 34%		
Late majority (two years of pandemic-altered schooling) ≈ 34%		
Laggards ≈ 16%		

INVEST WISELY IN A SCHOOLWIDE APPROACH

Impacting the emotional regulation skills of students requires a thoughtful examination of what the intended outcomes should be. This is sometimes skipped in the rush to adopt a new set of practices schoolwide. The attention is placed wholly on the features of a curriculum or set of procedures without first attending to what the intended outcomes should be. The evidence on the implementation of any school- or district-wide initiate is straightforward: without a shared vision and shared agreements, even the best-designed program is doomed to fail.

> *Without a shared vision and shared agreements, even the best-designed program is doomed to fail.*

Decisions about implementing emotional regulation instruction and practices, such as *identifying emotions* and assisting students with self-management, require discussion with the educators at the school about purpose and outcomes. A frame we find useful for having these discussions relies on a backward planning approach. Although we are casting it in the context of decisions about an emotional regulation initiative, it can be flexibly utilized (McCawley, n.d.):

1. What is the problem we intend to impact?

2. What will it look like when we achieve the desired outcome?

3. What teacher behaviors need to change for that outcome to be achieved?

4. What knowledge or skills do teachers need before their behaviors will change?

5. What activities do teachers need to engage in for their professional learning?

6. What resources will be required to achieve the desired outcome?

These questions can be utilized by smaller groups as well, such as a grade level or a professional learning community. Discussion of these questions allows space for educators to think through outcomes and changes necessary, and not simply move directly to professional development and resources.

NOTE TO SELF

We invite you to consider these same questions in light of a possible emotional regulation initiative at your school. This is intended to be a precursor to a larger group discussion. Therefore, the responses we ask you to complete now are at the level of self. What do you believe to be the rationale for such an effort? We then invite you to later consider these with a group of colleagues.

REFLECTIVE QUESTION	WHAT I THINK	WHAT WE THINK
What is the problem we intend to impact?		
What will it look like when we achieve the desired outcome?		
What teacher behaviors need to change for that outcome to be achieved?		
What knowledge or skills do teachers need before their behaviors will change?		
What activities do teachers need to engage in for their professional learning?		
What resources will be required to achieve the desired outcome?		

CASE IN POINT

The staff of Desert Wind Elementary School (DWES) is exploring different possibilities for bringing in self-regulation as a schoolwide focus. They have seen that their children struggle more than they have in the past with emotional outbursts and negative emotions. A core belief of this school has been that taking care of the emotional lives of children makes it possible for them to blossom. The DWES parent-teacher organization has a long record of working in tandem with the staff and community to support new initiatives. A representative coalition of staff and parents has decided that they will begin by conducting a survey to gain a sense of what the needs might be. Develop three questions for surveys of staff, students, and parents.

THREE QUESTIONS FOR A STAFF SURVEY	THREE QUESTIONS FOR A STUDENT SURVEY	THREE QUESTIONS FOR A FAMILY SURVEY
1.	1.	1.
2.	2.	2.
3.	3.	3.

Perhaps there is no more suitable module for self-assessment than one dedicated to emotional regulation. Revisit the major concepts and practices profiled in this module and use the traffic light scale to determine where you are now in each practice.

Menu of Practices on Emotional Regulation

Use the traffic light scale to reflect on your current practices as they relate to emotional regulation at the levels of self, students, and school. What areas do you want to strengthen?

INDIVIDUAL OPPORTUNITIES	
I can recognize situations when I can apply emotional self-regulation techniques.	●————————————●
I can strategically up-regulate or down-regulate to improve my emotional responses.	●————————————●
I am balancing internal and external self-awareness to strengthen relationships.	●————————————●
STUDENT-LEVEL OPPORTUNITIES	
I have strategies or I can improve existing strategies I have for assisting students in identifying emotions.	●————————————●
I have the tools to help students manage their emotions in ways that are humane and growth producing.	●————————————●
I routinely consider the emotional lives of my students, not just their behavior, when problems arise.	●————————————●
SCHOOL-LEVEL APPROACHES	
I can apply a backward planning technique to improve implementation decisions at my school or district.	●————————————●
I can better discern the emotional lives and support needs of my colleagues.	●————————————●

What do I need to do to change my reds to yellows?

Who can support me to turn my yellows into greens?

How am I using my greens to positively contribute to the good of the whole?

  Access resources, tools, and guides for this module at
resources.corwin.com/theselplaybook

MODULE 4

....

RELATIONAL TRUST
AND COMMUNICATION

wordclouds.com

BUILDING BACKGROUND

"Relational trust," wrote Bryk and Schneider (2002), "is the connective tissue that holds improving schools together" (p. 144). Their work with Chicago Public Schools points to a condition common in the successful schools they studied: trust is at the core. The collective work of these schools was focused on improving student achievement. Those schools that had high levels of trust among staff, students, and families made steady gains over 10 years.

Each school is a complex brew of human relationships that can either elevate or diminish the learning of individuals and groups. These interdependent relationships are formed within and across groups. Some of these interdependent relationships are symmetrical, meaning that the power of each member is similar. For example, teacher-teacher and student-student relationships are fueled by the *relational trust* they have for one another as equals. Other interdependent relationships are asymmetrical, meaning that there is a power differential. Teacher-student relationships and those between administrators and teachers require relational trust and communication that requires taking the perspective of the other person as well as an understanding of oneself (Warren, 2018). If you are hearing the echoes of concepts in previous modules, especially emotional intelligence and social capital, you are exactly right. Relational trust impacts each and links them all—connective tissue, indeed.

> Each school is a complex brew of human relationships that can either elevate or diminish the learning of individuals and groups.

Relational trust must be nurtured and not left up to chance. Our work as educators requires that we work with all our colleagues, students, and their families, not just those with whom we have forged a personal bond. Some of these are symmetrical while others are asymmetrical, but relational trust is both a lubricant to the work and "a moral resource for the hard work of local school improvement" (Bryk, 2010, p. 27). In other words, having trust in others becomes an asset you can draw upon, especially when there is disagreement.

In the educational space, notes Bryk, relational trust occurs as a result of the following:

- **Mutual respect** between parties, especially when there is disagreement or conflict
- **Personal regard** demonstrated through warmth and caring about others (openness, sharing personal stories, gentle humor—these are ways in which we show our personal regard for others)
- **Competence in core responsibilities,** as each member of the school community has specific role responsibilities, and all are in turn dependent on one another's competent execution of those duties (*what does it mean to be a great teacher/student/leader/family at our school?*)
- **Personal integrity,** the final component of relational trust and a function of a person's honesty and reliability; the fundamental measure of how we determine whether a person deserves our trust (in an educational setting, this is perceiving that colleagues have the welfare of students in mind)

The Role of Empathy

These are characteristics of relational trust in schools, and they are fostered and maintained by an empathic mindset. *Empathy* is at once "emotional (empathic concern) and cognitive (perspective taking)" notes Warren (2018, p. 171). We experience empathic concern as an emotional response to another who is in need. Empathy is not the same as sympathy, which is sadness for another person's experience. Empathy is an emotion borne of compassion and a desire to help.

It is also a response that involves thinking and reasoning through *perspective taking*. When we take the perspective of another person, we're better able to understand how a situation appears to another person and how this might be influencing their own emotional and cognitive responses. The ability to consider a situation through another person's view, particularly one that is not the same as yours, is key to resolving conflict and disagreement.

> *Empathic concern is associated with administrators' ability to be social justice leaders.*

The ability of teachers to adopt empathic concern and perspective taking is linked to their ability to enact culturally responsive pedagogies (Warren, 2018). "Adopting the social perspectives of others as an act and process of knowing," the researcher writes, "invites [teachers] to obtain (and reason with) new knowledge of students and the sociocultural context where they teach" (p. 169).

Similarly, empathic concern and perspective taking are associated with administrators' ability to be social justice leaders (Boske et al., 2017). Empathy was at the core of leaders' skills to develop culturally responsive self-knowledge, co-create inclusive practices for all students, and engage with diverse school communities. One leader, reflecting on her own work on developing perspective taking, stated:

> When I started to think about what it meant to live on the margins and really work with people who were disenfranchised, I found myself being concerned about the welfare of my children, their families, and society . . . my thoughts and my actions shifted, and I tried to engage with people in new ways and learn from them rather than thinking they had something to learn from me . . . I was being present in a whole new way. (p. 381)

Listening, being present, demonstrating concern, and taking action—these skills center on how we strengthen ourselves, our students, and our schools. Take another look at your VIA-IS Character Strengths Profile that you developed in Module 1. Empathic concern and perspective taking are manifested across several strengths, including *perspective, teamwork, judgment, social intelligence,* and *leadership*. Are any of these signature strengths for you?

Relational trust is driven by investment in communication tools and social skills that allow for individuals and groups to act from a position of concern and perspective taking. In this module, you will learn how to

- Develop your own trustworthiness and credibility

- Invest in students' relational trust with you and with peers

- Develop relational trust with families

VOCABULARY SELF-AWARENESS

Directions: Consider the terms below.

- If it is new to you, write the date in the Level 1 column.
- If you have heard the word before but are not sure that you can use it in a sentence or define it, write the date in the Level 2 column.
- If this word is very familiar to you and you can define it and use it in a sentence, write the date in the Level 3 column.

Update your understanding of the terms as you engage in this module and in your work. Note that there are spaces for you to add terms that are new to you.

WORD	LEVEL 1	LEVEL 2	LEVEL 3	SENTENCE	DEFINITION
Relational trust					
Empathy					
Perspective taking					
Practical trust					
Emotional trust					
Social cohesion					
Teacher credibility					

WORD	LEVEL 1	LEVEL 2	LEVEL 3	SENTENCE	DEFINITION
Peer relationships					
Communication skills					
Family voice					
Family decision making					

Level 1 = This word is new to me.

Level 2 = I have heard this word before.

Level 3 = I know the definition and I can use it in a sentence!

CASEL Connections for educators, students, and schools in this module:

SELF-AWARENESS	SELF-MANAGEMENT	SOCIAL AWARENESS	RELATIONSHIP SKILLS	RESPONSIBLE DECISION MAKING
Trustworthiness		Empathy	Relational trust	Family voice
Teacher credibility		Perspective taking	Practical and emotional trust	Family decision making
			Communication skills	
			Social cohesion	

RELATIONAL TRUST AND COMMUNICATION BEGIN WITH SELF

The productive work of teams thrives in a climate of trust. As educators, we are integral members of any number of teams—department or grade level, professional learning communities, committees—that require a level of relational trust to operate. Teams that have low trust find that their own work is undermined, despite their efforts. Members of teams with low trust experience higher levels of stress and lower levels of job satisfaction.

A simple definition of *trust* involves truth and reliability of information. But when it comes to complex organizations like schools, the definition of trust is more complex. We have adopted the definition of trust proposed by Hoy and Tschannen-Moran (2003): "Trust is an individual's or group's willingness to be vulnerable to another party based on the confidence that the latter party is benevolent, reliable, competent, honest, and open" (p. 189). We appreciate this definition because it acknowledges that we must be vulnerable if we are to develop trust. And that goes for students as well as our professional peers.

The decision to trust is based on the signals received from others. Now, turn that back to oneself: *How am I signaling that I am trustworthy?* The trustworthiness of an individual stems from two dimensions: *practical trust* and *emotional trust*. Practical trust has to do with reliability. People who enjoy high levels of practical trust show up on time and complete the work they have promised in a timely way. Emotional trust requires that you demonstrate care and respect for others, speak and act with integrity, admit when you're wrong, and demonstrate the "confident vulnerability" that creates a space for others to do the same. To be confidently vulnerable is to disclose details about your first year at the school to a new team member. A confidently vulnerable instructional coach shares a personal anecdote about the difficulty they faced when first implementing a new strategy. A principal who is confidently vulnerable advises her assistant principal about errors in her own career that she hopes they'll avoid.

NOTE TO SELF

How do you convey that you are trustworthy practically and emotionally?

	I DO THIS OFTEN.	I SOMETIMES DO THIS.	I RARELY, IF EVER, DO THIS.
PRACTICAL TRUST			
I arrive early to scheduled meetings.			
I keep track of my work obligations so I get them done.			
My completed work is timely and accurate.			

	I DO THIS OFTEN.	I SOME-TIMES DO THIS.	I RARELY, IF EVER, DO THIS.
EMOTIONAL TRUST			
I take the time to demonstrate care for others.			
I convey my respect for others through my words and actions.			
The information I share with others is accurate.			
When I am wrong, I admit it to my team.			
I do not share gossip or tear down others who are not present.			
I volunteer to help whenever I am able.			
I explain myself so that my intentions are understood by others.			
I allow myself to be confidently vulnerable to others.			

Now analyze your practical and emotional trust behaviors. Which are areas of strength? What growth opportunities do you see?

MY STRENGTHS	MY GROWTH OPPORTUNITIES

INVEST IN COMMUNICATING YOUR TRUSTWORTHINESS

You have probably already noted that much of your ability to convey your trustworthiness is a function of how you communicate. Many of the formally structured interactions mandated by the school (e.g., grade or department meetings, professional learning communities) result in what Newberry et al. (2018) call *contrived relationships*. These meetings have an "administrative focus [but] lack the emotional depth that teachers need to support the emotion work they perform daily" (p. 33). They note that without attention to the emotional subtext of these interactions, deeper working relationships are inhibited due to differing practices and philosophies. Members are therefore reluctant to share ideas or beliefs, as they have been encouraged to "relate to one another as 'educators' rather than as fellow human beings" (Shapiro, 2007, p. 618).

> We must be vulnerable if we are to develop trust.

The communication tools pioneered by Costa and Garmston's (2015) work on cognitive coaching are invaluable for conveying your trustworthiness to colleagues (and students, too). Learn more about their seven norms of collaborative work at this book's companion website, resources.corwin.com/theselplaybook.

NOTE TO SELF

How do you convey that you are trustworthy in your communication?

	I OFTEN DO THIS.	I SOME-TIMES DO THIS.	I RARELY OR NEVER DO THIS.
PAUSING			
I refrain from speaking over others.			
I allow time when the speaker finishes before adding information.			
PARAPHRASING			
I acknowledge the ideas of others.			
I avoid using I-statements when paraphrasing.			
POSING QUESTIONS			
I ask clarifying questions when I need additional details.			
I ask open-ended questions to mediate the speaker's thinking.			

	I OFTEN DO THIS.	I SOME-TIMES DO THIS.	I RARELY OR NEVER DO THIS.
PROVIDING DATA			
My conversations about data are neutral.			
I keep the discussion focused on the data.			
PUTTING IDEAS ON THE TABLE			
I use neutral language to separate ideas from people.			
I focus on the ideas on the table rather than on who suggested the idea.			
PAYING ATTENTION TO SELF AND OTHERS			
I monitor my personal reactions to ideas and people.			
I notice the behaviors and actions of others to gain understanding of their mood.			
PRESUME POSITIVE INTENTIONS			
I work to maintain and enhance relational trust.			
I reframe statements of others such that they convey a presumption of positive intentions.			

Now analyze your communication skills for conveying trustworthiness. Which are areas of strength? What growth opportunities do you see?

MY STRENGTHS	MY GROWTH OPPORTUNITIES

CASE IN POINT

It's before the start of a new school year, and the science teachers at Cherry Middle School (CMS) have decided to meet to map out their department goals for the year, catch up on how everyone's summer was, and get to know the newest member of the team, Stephen Perry.

Mr. Perry is a seasoned science teacher and has taught for several years in a different part of the state. He recently moved to the area and is excited to start the year at CMS. Although Mr. Perry is new, he is eager to contribute to the team and provide input as they set their goals, and he shares experiences from his previous district. The department meeting goes pretty well, and the team sets some solid goals for the year.

Over the course of the semester, conversations between Mr. Perry and his colleagues frequently include references to his previous district and school. He often uses phrases such as "It wasn't like this in my old district," "Last year I . . . ," or "When I was at my old school. . . ." Mr. Perry is clearly having difficulty adjusting to teaching at Cherry, and his colleagues begin to tire of hearing about his previous school and gradually fade away from seeking out interaction with him unless it's during staff or department meetings. As a result, Mr. Perry adopts the attitude that it's just best to close his door and do things the way he wants rather than seek help or advice from his peers.

How could the science teachers have worked to build a better relationship with Mr. Perry in order to support his transition to the new school?	
What could Mr. Perry have done differently in this scenario?	

RELATIONAL TRUST AND COMMUNICATION ARE FOSTERED WITH AND AMONG STUDENTS

If you've taught for more than two years, you have likely experienced the phenomenon that no two classes are ever alike. The grade level, subject, and school setting may remain the same, but the brew of student personalities makes each group unique. We broadly refer to this as the *classroom community*, but that community is greatly impacted by the social cohesion of the group. *Social cohesion* refers to "positive interpersonal relations between students, a sense of belonging of all students, and group solidarity" (Veerman & Denessen, 2021). In other words, how does this particular group of young people communicate, resolve problems, and learn together? Do members feel a sense of belonging? Do they have a sense of the common good? With an effect size of 0.53, a cohesive group of students who work together with the teacher toward positive learning goals is much more likely to achieve its goals (visiblelearningmetax.com). As a result, strong social cohesion has the potential to accelerate the learning of the members of the group.

The social cohesion of the classroom doesn't have to be left up to chance. While the personalities and prior experiences of the individuals will vary, you have the ability to directly impact and foster the cohesion needed for optimal learning conditions. Invest in the relational trust of the classroom and the social skills of its members.

INVEST IN RELATIONAL TRUST OF STUDENTS

The climate of the classroom, which is to say the psychological, social, and emotional learning environment, has a significant influence on the academic lives of its members. Although definitions of climate vary, most agree that it is an amalgamation of three factors that together contribute to relational trust:

- Teacher-student relationships
- Peer relationships
- Learning opportunities, supports, and management (Toren & Seginer, 2015)

First, teacher-student relationships need to be cultivated with intention. The quality of these relationships correlates with the trust students have in their teacher, which in turn determines how open they are to instruction and feedback. We are not talking about adults being "friends" with students; in fact, we think such an approach is counterproductive and inauthentic. Rather, effective teacher-student relationships are built on a foundation of respect for the young person as an individual and a learner. A truly enormous yet rarely discussed quality of teacher-student relationships is the perceived credibility of the teacher in the eyes of the student. The influence of *teacher credibility* on student learning, with an effect size of 1.09, puts it in the top 10 of the 322 influences identified in the Visible Learning database (visiblelearningmetax.com). Teacher credibility is linked to students' belief that they can learn from this person. There are four characteristics we can cultivate to be credible to our students:

- **Competence:** "Do I believe my teacher possesses the content knowledge and an understanding of my learning as a student?"

- **Trustworthiness:** "Do I see my teacher as benevolent? Is my teacher reliable and honest?"

- **Dynamism:** "Is my teacher passionate about the subject they teach, and enthusiastic about being here with us?"

- **Immediacy:** "Is my teacher warm and caring? Does my teacher respond positively when my classmates or I struggle academically or emotionally?"

In order to foster relational trust with students, we must model what it looks like and feels like each day. Conscious attention to our own credibility as educators shows students through actions how a caring classroom operates. The investment we make in fostering our relationships with individual students has a further signaling effect on other students. When we demonstrate a positive and caring relationship for a student, we positively impact the perception by peers of the student's worthiness.

To be sure, it isn't always easy to build a relationship with a student. Some are more remote, and we don't know them well. In other cases, we might not feel as much affinity for an individual (we are human, after all). But we don't just teach the students we immediately like; we owe it to each one to develop a positive learning relationship with them, and this requires consciously interrupting our own interaction patterns. A favorite technique is the 2 × 10 approach, developed by Wlodkowski and Ginsberg (1995), for starting or jumpstarting a relationship with a student. The premise is simple: commit to having a casual conversation for 2 minutes a day, for 10 days in a row. Don't notify the student of your plan; just find ways to talk to the student, especially about things that aren't directly related to school. Find out what they're interested in, or ask them for a recommendation about something they are knowledgeable about. If you work in a big school, you might need to hold these talks right before or after class. These can be held in the hallway during passing period, in the lunchroom, or on the playground. In the process, you may discover something about yourself. The interesting thing about relationships is that they go both ways—your intentional communication with a student fosters your own feelings of warmth and caring for the student.

NOTE TO SELF

Reflect on your relationships with your students. Who have you had more difficulty establishing a positive teacher-student relationship with? Use the table to plan your 2 × 10 conversations. At the end of the two weeks, note what it is that you have learned about the student. How will you use this knowledge to strengthen your relationship?

2 × 10 plan for _____

Time period: _____

PLANNING QUESTIONS	IDEAS	WHAT I LEARNED	HOW I WILL USE IT
Logistics: when and where?			
What do I want to know more about this student?			
Possible topics			

INVEST IN PEER RELATIONSHIPS AND COMMUNICATION SKILLS

The second dimension of social cohesion is in the *peer relationships* students have with one another. This proves to be a rockier road for some than for others, and the academic and behavioral difficulties they have in the classroom can negatively impact the relationship they have with peers. Those students who have disruptive behaviors are especially vulnerable. One study demonstrated that students with disruptive behaviors had declining relationships with peers that persisted nine months later (Mikami et al., 2012).

Students who have disruptive behaviors are especially vulnerable.

Of course, peer relationships are not unrelated to the teacher. These same disruptive students often have a negative relationship with their teacher, too. In fact, the teacher's response to disruptive behaviors can positively or negatively influence the social preferences of classmates. Students are really good at figuring out who the teacher dislikes; our negative reactions telegraph how we expect our students to react. The result? "My teacher doesn't like Emily, and I don't, either." On the other hand, teachers who provided emotional and instructional support for disruptive students and who did not promote an academic status hierarchy in the classroom reduced the negative social rejection of disruptive students by their peers (Mikami et al., 2012). Avoid practices that highlight the comparative achievement of students, such as

- Visual displays of the academic progress of all the students in the class (e.g., number of books read, current reading or mathematics levels, test results)

- Visual displays of behavioral achievement (e.g., clip charts)

- Differential award systems (e.g., table points, class points)

- Consistent student grouping by achievement levels (e.g., tracking, permanent homogeneous groups, ability grouping)

The great news about peer relationships is that they can have a significant positive effect. Positive peer influences, which are growth producing, have an effect size of 0.53 on learning (visiblelearningmetax.com). Positive peer influences can increase physical activity and reduce risky behaviors, including smoking, substance abuse, and other behaviors that cause health-related concerns. In addition, they can increase the likelihood of young people's pursuits of their aspirations through post-secondary college and career education. And peer acceptance is not limited to friendships; rather, it is a measure of the extent to which a young person is liked and welcomed in activities and tasks, regardless of friendship (Wentzel et al., 2021).

Students are really good at figuring out who the teacher dislikes.

PROMOTE COMMUNICATION SKILLS

Peer relationships among students are nurtured and hampered by their ability to communicate with one another. For young children in the classroom, this often takes the form of listening and speaking procedures. Importantly, these protocols should evolve over the school year so that students' ability to sustain a conversation grows. For instance, kindergarten partner talk in a classroom is shaped by higher expectations as the year progresses, from Level 1 to Level 4 (see Figure 4.1).

Build students' *communication skills* with language frames that provide students with the support they need to work together respectfully and productively. Students may not have the vocabulary for the give-and-take needed as they work through an academic problem, so teach and model the use of the language frames in your classroom and make them visible to learners. It is useful to post them as table tents to remind students to use them. Examples of language frames include

- My answer is _____ because _____. I think the answer is _____ because _____. I agree with _____, however, _____. _____ can be also shown as _____.

- Why did you choose that operation? [clarification in math]

- I chose that operation because _____. [justifying the solution in math]

- I think _____ belongs in this category because _____. What do you think?

FIGURE 4.1 PARTNER TALK RUBRIC

SOURCE: Created using Canva.com.

- Can you explain how/why _____?

- I wonder what would happen if _____.

- Let's find out how we can test our idea for _____.

- I agree _____ because _____.

- I disagree _____ because _____.

- What do you think will happen if _____ happens next?

- After listening to _____ I found that _____.

- Why do you think _____?

- How did _____ change _____?

Communication is also nonverbal and can easily be misunderstood by others. One's body language, tone, volume, facial expressions, gestures, and proximity convey not only ideas but also emotions. In fact, people often describe the nonverbal signals they receive from others as being a way to "read" someone's thoughts and mood, and these signals can be subject to cultural interpretations. Eye contact can easily be misinterpreted as aggressive or disrespectful, especially when there is an age difference, such as when a child is speaking to an adult. While students are commonly told to make eye contact with others, this can be a challenge for some who have been taught to avert their eyes as a sign of respect.

Some facial expressions are universal, such as those that convey anger, sadness, or joy. Many gestures, which are called speech illustrators, are universal as well (think of it as "talking with your hands"), although there is variance in the amount used, which can vary according to gender and culture (Matsumoto et al., 2012). Young children and students with communication difficulties can benefit from lessons that associate various facial expressions with emotions and how to respond to them. Students of all ages can profit from tips about body language in groups, such as proximity and position. A student who is sitting away from her table group with her arms crossed is definitely projecting her dissatisfaction with her peers or perhaps with the situation. Rather than just moving to correct the outward nonverbal behavior, find out what's happening. If you learn that everything really is okay, it may be appropriate to share a quiet reminder with the student about how her nonverbals aren't matching her message.

The verbal and nonverbal communication skills needed to establish and maintain positive peer relationships are not learned in a single sitting. Make sure to weave these into the fabric of the classroom; you possess a great deal of influence on peer relationships. The National Center on Safe Supportive Learning Environments makes the following recommendations for investing in peer relationships in your classroom.

TEACHER RECOMMENDATIONS FOR PROMOTING PEER RELATIONSHIPS	HOW
1. Teach students positive social interactions daily during large group activities. Any group time in class usually provides good opportunities to take a few minutes to teach these skills.	• Explain the social skill. • Demonstrate the correct way to use it. • Provide an incorrect example or nonexample and let students figure out what step was missing. • Let a student practice a skill with an adult. • Let a student practice a skill with another student. • Refresh the skill (or provide "boosters") by repeating the skill in later situations.

2. Monitor class time for naturally occurring, positive peer social interactions. Actively move around the classroom, interact with students during activities, and look for students who are using the targeted social skills. Be ready to provide assistance, support, and direction to promote successful peer interactions among students.	• Provide cueing as needed by reminding students to
	  o Work together.
	  o Share materials and ideas.
	  o Be persistent.
	  o Practice active listening.
	  o Monitor their nonverbal behaviors.

TEACHER RECOMMENDATIONS FOR PROMOTING PEER RELATIONSHIPS	HOW
3. Provide additional assistance to students, as needed, to ensure that peer social interactions are successful.	• Model the appropriate behavior. • Give specific verbal cues (e.g., "remember to tap him on the shoulder"). • Provide physical assistance. • Create opportunities for students to talk about the social skill.
4. Affirm students who are using targeted social skills with positive feedback and attention. Offer encouragement or support.	• Provide positive feedback and attention on the use of the social skills. • Name the skill and the ways in which it was being used. • Recognize students individually for their use of the skill in a variety of settings.

SOURCE: Adapted from National Center on Safe Supportive Learning Environments (n.d.).

CASE IN POINT

Norma Hamasaki has taught first grade for more than 15 years. Although she knows the importance of developing students' social and communication skills, specific instruction related to this topic has never taken center stage in her classroom. She has occasionally read picture books aloud and has periodic lessons and activities to address important skills, such as using kind language, taking turns, listening, and following directions. Often, the need for these activities and lessons has come reactively rather than proactively.

As a result of the pandemic, however, Ms. Hamasaki is seeing the need to devote more time and attention to helping students develop their social skills than in years past. She has noticed that in addition to the "typical first-grade behaviors," her students need significant support with skills such as having patience, working with others, and appropriate behavior when circumstances are different than expected. Although reading children's literature books has helped and is typically a good anchor for Ms. Hamasaki to start with, she has begun to use role playing as a key strategy to help her students practice the skills they need to develop.

(Continued)

(Continued)

She begins by reading a scenario aloud to her class. They discuss the scenario and create a T-chart to brainstorm appropriate ways as well as inappropriate ways to handle the situation. Then she selects students to participate in multiple rounds of role play. This way, lots of students get to practice building their skills, their confidence, and their language appropriate to the scenario. Sometimes she prompts the students to use ideas from their list of appropriate responses during their role play. Other times, she prompts the students to use ideas from their list of inappropriate responses. After each round of role playing, the class has a whole-group discussion to share what they saw (encouraging attention to both verbal and nonverbal cues), ask questions, and reflect on how the scenario either helped or hurt those involved.

How does the process Ms. Hamasaki uses for role playing help the students develop social skills? What further recommendations can you make to her about promoting social skills? Use the chart from the National Center on Safe Supportive Learning Environments on pages 108–109 to support your thinking.

RELATIONAL TRUST AND COMMUNICATION ARE NURTURED BY SCHOOLS

What about families? In previous sections of this module, we have highlighted the need for relational trust, social skills, and communication in our interactions with colleagues and our students. But an essential component of the social and emotional health of the members of an organization lies in its relationship with families. Family-school partnerships are widely understood as a key to the academic and social-emotional growth of students, and there is a relationship between parent involvement and student learning, with a 0.42 effect size (visiblelearning.com). Indeed, parent involvement has one of the most extensive of all the influences in the Visible Learning database, representing 1.2 million students.

> Family-school partnerships are widely understood as a key to the academic and social-emotional growth of students.

The problem, however, is that conventional family involvement efforts often align more to American middle-class expectations, such as volunteering at school. This doesn't reflect the needs and realities of most families today, either economically or culturally. There are far fewer full-time stay-at-home parents who can volunteer during the school day. And, of course, narrow definitions of involvement like these don't begin to address cultural and language expectations of families. Notably, many schools are unaware of the broad range of child-rearing practices and arrangements represented in their community (Davidson & Case, 2018). Overall, a school's well-meaning but misguided efforts narrowly focus on "making home more like school, rather than school more like home" (Frey, 2010, p. 42). In order to strengthen family-school partnerships, Davidson and Case (2018) recommend that schools take the following actions:

- Develop trust and relationships
- Elevate the voice of marginalized families
- Share decision-making power

INVEST IN RELATIONAL TRUST WITH FAMILIES

Establishing a relationship with a family requires rapport. Many families will tell you they never hear from their child's school unless there is a problem. Interrupt this cycle by creating some practices that make it possible to meet families where they are, literally and figuratively. Some teachers make a point of sending a message to their new students in the weeks before school starts. This is a lovely practice, to be sure, and most children like getting something in the mail from a teacher they have as yet to meet. But are these practices carried forward? Some students start school long after the opening of the school year. Are those children and their families personally contacted? You can imagine how much more fraught the idea of attending a new school is going to be for a young person who is starting at the midpoint of the academic year. A friendly note or phone call is likely to be welcome for a stressed family.

Home visits can be a useful way to establish rapport. At the school where the three of us work, students with disabilities and their families are contacted by the special educator to welcome them to the school. They offer to meet with the family at their home, or at another location if the family prefers (not everyone wants you in their house). The special educator hosts an informal interview with the student and family to learn more about the student in an effort to create supports that are aligned with the student's and the family's expectations. This has proven to be an excellent way to get to know students who are new to the school and to establish a trusting relationship with the family. A version of the student profile form can be found in Figure 4.2.

FIGURE 4.2 STUDENT PROFILE

Student Name:
Date:
Profile Completed By:
Persons Interviewed:
What are this student's areas of strengths and interest?
What aspirations does this student have?
What have been some successful learning strategies and adaptations?
Does this student use any informal or formal communication strategies?
What positive behavioral support strategies really seem to work?
Are there assessment accommodations?
Is there important family or health information we should know about?

Another important technique for establishing rapport and relational trust is through attendance at community events. Representation by the school at local festivals and public events is always appreciated. Many administrators make it a point to attend these events because they offer the opportunity to get to know families in their own spaces. Too often, the expectation is for the family to come to us, rather than us going to them.

It is crucial to know the needs of the school community and its families in order to create responsive systems. Our own work with schools has included partnering with other agencies to establish a school-based health center and offering English-language courses for families at no cost to them. In both cases, these were driven by needs families had identified.

> Too often, the expectation is for the family to come to us, rather than us going to them.

At the school where we currently work, we have put procedures in place, consistent with California school law, for a family safety plan in the event that a student's caregiver is detained by Immigration and Customs Enforcement for deportation. We relied on the wisdom of families to help us craft those procedures. They advised us to include information in the family safety plan, encouraging families in need to file a caregiver's authorization affidavit to award temporary custody should this occur, and connected us with an immigration attorney who could further advise us.

Relational trust begins with establishing rapport but truly blossoms when schools take steps to learn about the community, its strengths, and its gifts as well as needs. These partnerships, in turn, expand the school's resources to support children.

 NOTE TO SELF

What efforts do you or your colleagues participate in to build rapport and relational trust with families?

Initial introductions to families new to the school	
Home or community visits to become acquainted (not just problem solving)	
School representation at community events	
Soliciting advice from families about community needs	

INVEST IN FAMILY VOICE AND DECISION MAKING

Schools that commit to nurturing trust with families ensure that there is a place at the table for them to have a voice in school decision making. And just as importantly, we need them to do so. As Davidson and Case (2018) note, "when families' voices are valued, they are more likely to step into leadership roles in the school community" (p. 53). The National Parent–Teacher Association offers guidelines for developing and maintaining ways for schools and families to work together in healthy and beneficial ways:

- **Welcoming all families into the school community** requires not only that schools create a productive climate but also that families are welcoming of one another. An inclusive climate depends on every member, including those with differing cultural, racial, economic, and family structures.

- **Effectively communicating** such that information is shared with one another, and that families seek to be active and engaged members of the school community. This looks different for every family and is not limited to those who are able to volunteer. Effective communication means that ideas and input are offered for the common good.

- **Supporting student success** requires that families provide children with the social, emotional, psychological, and physical nurturing that makes it possible for the school to build academic learning.

- **Speaking up for every child** extends the previous standard. Families advocate for those who struggle to meet the needs of their children and partner with the school to attend to the needs of the most vulnerable.

- **Sharing power** means that democratic principles of schooling are embodied in a willingness to debate ideas, listen to one another, and find win-win solutions.

Having said that, too often families are limited to narrow lanes rather than allowed to be full participants in the school community. Consider a range of experiences that families have when it comes to involvement in their child's school. We've arranged them from lesser opportunities for family voice to those where family voice is an essential part of the school.

- **Expression:** Family involvement is minimal and superficial.

- **Consultation:** Family opinions are gathered when school personnel initiate.

- **Participation:** Families are observers of meetings directed by school personnel.

- **Partnership:** Families are formal members of committees, and families receive professional learning on working in these venues.

- **Activism:** Families identify problems and generate solutions to address issues in the school and the community.

- **Leadership:** Families lead these efforts, co-planning with and directing school personnel.

Take an account of the opportunities for *family voice* and *decision making* at your school. We have adapted Toshalis and Nakkula's (2012) work on student voice in schools to frame family voice and decision making. Make sure that families are represented in your assessment. Where do you see yourselves currently? How might you grow?

Current Stage on the Spectrum: _____

CURRENT STRENGTHS	GROWTH OPPORTUNITIES

A Spectrum of Family Voice–Oriented Activity

Families articulating their perspectives ← - - - - - - - - → **Families involved as stakeholders** - - - - - - - - → Families directing collective activities

Families as data sources ← - - - - - - - - → **Families as collaborators** - - - - - - - - → Families as leaders of change

EXPRESSION	CONSULTATION	PARTICIPATION	PARTNERSHIP	ACTIVISM	LEADERSHIP
Volunteering opinions, creating art, celebrating, complaining, praising, objecting	Being asked for their opinion, providing feedback, serving on a focus group, completing a survey	Attending meetings or events in which decisions are made, frequent inclusion when issues are framed, and actions planned	Formalized role in decision making, standard operations require (not just invite) family involvement, educators are trained in how to work collaboratively with family partners	Identifying problems, generating solutions, organizing responses, agitating and/or educating for change both in and outside of school contexts	(Co-)planning, making decisions and accepting significant responsibility for outcomes, (co-)guiding group processes, (co-)conducting activities

Most family-voice activity in schools/classrooms resides at this end of the spectrum.

The need for adults to share authority, demonstrate trust, protect against co-optation, learn from each other, and handle disagreement increases from left to right. Families' influence, responsibility, and decision-making roles increase from left to right.

SOURCE: Adapted from Toshalis and Nakkula (2012, p. 24).

CASE IN POINT

Oakwood High School is the oldest school in the district, with a long history of achievement in sports and academics. It boasts the largest alumni association of all the schools in the region, which has traditionally been fueled by its sports legacy. However, the constituents it serves currently are quite different from those who attended the school in the 1960s. What had been historically a predominantly white, working-class community 50 years ago has transformed into a neighborhood of people from all over the world. Local churches and mosques have worked with city and state officials to host refugees from places experiencing conflict. One administrator said, "If [a country] is in the headlines, we'll soon have their families here."

However, the school has been slow to figure out how to build relational trust and communication with many of the families it serves. The alumni association, which is the major contributor to the school's foundation, has been accustomed to having an influence on school decisions, but some of their recent decisions have been out of step with the community's needs and desires.

The leadership team wants to strengthen their ability to build ties and be responsive to a vibrant school community. How might you advise them about doing so? Use the chart below to guide your advice for Oakwood.

ISSUES AND DILEMMAS	YOUR ADVICE
Learning about current community strengths and needs	
Increasing the school's visibility in the community	

ISSUES AND DILEMMAS	YOUR ADVICE
Developing family voice in school operations	
Learning about alumni association's concerns	
Fostering community partnerships	
Leveraging local government and nonprofit resources	

SELF-ASSESSMENT

Revisit the major concepts and practices profiled in this module and use the traffic light scale to determine where you are now in each practice.

Menu of Practices on Trust, Social Skills, and Communication

Use the traffic light scale to reflect on your current practices about relational trust, social skills, and communication at the levels of self, students, and school. What areas do you want to strengthen?

INDIVIDUAL OPPORTUNITIES	
I am able to build my practical trust with others.	
I am able to build my emotional trust with others.	
I use communication tools to build my trustworthiness.	
STUDENT-LEVEL OPPORTUNITIES	
I invest in establishing and growing teacher-student relationships.	
I actively work on developing my teacher credibility.	
I teach and infuse peer relationships skills into my academics.	
I teach and infuse developmentally appropriate communication skills into my academics.	
SCHOOL-LEVEL APPROACHES	
I am knowledgeable about how my school or district invests in building relational trust with families.	
I see my own role in contributing to building relational trust with families.	
I advocate on the part of families to increase family voice in my school or district.	
I collaborate with families to make consequential decisions at the school.	

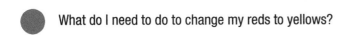

What do I need to do to change my reds to yellows?

Who can support me to turn my yellows into greens?

How am I using my greens to positively contribute to the good of the whole?

Access resources, tools, and guides for this module at
resources.corwin.com/theselplaybook

MODULE 5

····························

INDIVIDUAL AND
COLLECTIVE EFFICACY

BUILDING BACKGROUND

At the most basic level, efficacy is about the ability to produce the desired result. This requires that we define what the desired result is and then decide whether we believe that we have the ability to produce that result. Efficacy is a combination of defining the result or goal, mobilizing self-esteem, and recognizing the locus of control.

The goal or desired result is an important aspect of efficacy. If we do not care about the goal or are not motivated to achieve the goal, we are unlikely to exert effort toward that goal. For example, when students are presented with appropriately challenging goals that they value, the impact on their learning is strong. The effect size of appropriately challenging goals is 0.59, above average in terms of influence. Generally, there are two types of goals in school: performance and mastery. Performance goals compare one ability to others and are often focused on winning, looking smart, and getting good grades. The effect size of performance goals on learning is 0.03, pretty close to zero. Alternatively, mastery goals focus on learning and completing a task according to a set of standards. The effect size for mastery goals is 0.13, better but not that powerful. What seems to make a difference is students committing to the goals, which increases the impact to 0.40, and clarity of the goal or desired result, which has an effect size of 0.51.

That's a lot of information that may seem contradictory. It seems that the type of goal is less important than students' understanding the goal (or result) and making a commitment to those results. We would argue the same holds true for educators and their school systems. Let's say, for example, that your desired result is better direct instruction and modeling for students. If you have clarity about what that means and you commit to it, you are much more likely to achieve the result. The same is true for school systems. Far too many of us have been told what the goals for the school are, such as a 10 percent increase in reading scores. Although that may seem worthwhile, if we lack clarity about what that means and we have other priorities, it is unlikely that we will achieve that goal.

Self-esteem is also an important aspect of efficacy. Coopersmith (1967) suggests that there are three indicators of self-esteem, including feelings of worth, feelings of ability, and feelings of acceptance. More specifically, these are as follows:

1. **Precious feelings:** A person's ability to see whether they are valuable to themselves and others around them.

2. **Feeling able:** A person's ability to see whether they are able to deal with difficulties, challenges, work, etc., at the level of solving the problem.

3. **Feeling received:** A person's ability to accept the strengths and weaknesses of themselves and others.

Each of these contributes to a person's efficacy and their ability to put forth the effort required to achieve the desired results. When any of these are compromised, the outcome is less likely to be realized. Of course, this also relates to a person's *locus of control*, a concept developed by Rotter (1954). People with a strong sense of an internal locus of control believe that things happen mainly as a result of their abilities, actions, or mistakes. People with a strong external locus of control believe that other forces, such as random chance, the environment, or other people, are responsible for the events that happen in their life. People tend to lean one way or the other. Those with an internal locus of control are generally more successful, healthier, and happier (e.g., Galvin et al., 2018). Here are some differences between the two:

INTERNAL LOCUS OF CONTROL	EXTERNAL LOCUS OF CONTROL
• Are more likely to take responsibility for their actions	• Blame outside forces for their circumstances
• Tend to be less influenced by the opinions of other people	• Often credit luck or chance for any successes
• Often do better at tasks when they are allowed to work at their own pace	• Don't believe that they can change their situation through their own efforts
• Usually have a strong sense of self-efficacy	• Frequently feel hopeless or powerless in the face of difficult situations
• Tend to work hard to achieve the things they want	• Are more prone to experiencing learned helplessness
• Feel confident in the face of challenges	
• Tend to be physically healthier	
• Report being happier and more independent	
• Often achieve greater success in the workplace	

SOURCE: Cherry (2020).

Importantly, these three aspects are not fixed and are part of our genetic make-up. They are, at least in part, influenced by the environment and our experiences. And they are malleable. Thus, we can change the ways in which we think about the desired results, develop self-esteem, and increase the sense of control we have in the world. This applies to our students and the school systems in which we work as well.

Together, these contribute to a sense of efficacy. Self-efficacy has a powerful influence on learning, with an effect size of 0.65. To date, there are 11 meta-analyses on self-efficacy representing 1,296,099 students. In other words, we're pretty confident that self-efficacy is an important consideration when it comes to learning. It's also an important way that young people come to terms with their adverse childhood experiences. Again, that's why social-emotional learning is as important as academic learning; they are interconnected and dependent on one another.

Bandura, the originator of the term, defined *self-efficacy* as our belief in our capacity to exercise control over our own functioning and over events that affect our lives. To put it in more simple terms, self-efficacy is our belief in our ability to succeed in a particular situation (Bandura, 1977). Note that this is different from confidence. We can be confident that we will fail. And we can be overconfident and actually unrealistic. Efficacy means that you can control your own motivation, behavior, and social environment. The four dimensions of efficacy are (Bandura, 1993):

1. **Experiences of mastery.** The experience of mastery is the single most important factor for developing and reinforcing efficacy. When we experience success through hard work or accomplishments, we begin to attribute those successes to our actions rather than outside forces. In other words, success breeds success. We look for situations in which we believe we will be successful because it reinforces our self-efficacy. Conversely, we tend to avoid situations in which we believe we will fail. Or, if we already have limited efficacy, we look for confirming evidence that we are not going to be successful.

2. **Modeling.** When we see others succeed, especially when we perceive them to be about the same as ourselves, our self-efficacy increases. To a large extent, people say to themselves, "If they can do it, so can I." Modeling experiences provide us with examples of what is possible. Importantly, these mastery experiences need to result in better outcomes if we are likely to try on that which was modeled for us.

3. **Social persuasion.** To a lesser extent, encouragement from others builds self-efficacy. We say to a lesser extent because the previous two factors are very powerful. But we don't want to ignore the power of peer support. When we trust the person who encourages us, we can increase our self-efficacy. If the person is honest with us and we believe that this person has our best interests at heart, social persuasion can serve as a tipping point.

> When we trust the person who encourages us, we can increase our self-efficacy.

4. **Physiological factors.** There are a number of physical and biological contributors to our self-efficacy. When we experience stress, our self-efficacy is generally reduced. That is, unless we learn to recognize that stress as part of a natural process. Similarly, when we are frightened, it's hard to maintain self-efficacy. Instead, we move into a flight, fight, or freeze situation. People with higher levels of self-efficacy recognize these physiological factors and understand that they are natural biological responses to situations that do not necessarily signal failure.

Figure 5.1 contains quotes from Bandura for each of these areas.

Maddux (2013) has suggested a fifth route to self-efficacy through *imaginal experiences*, or the art of visualizing yourself behaving effectively or successfully in a given situation. It's like the old saying that goes "it's so close you can almost taste it." Imaginal experiences require visualization and putting yourself (in your head) in the position of being capable of achieving what you intend to. As Maddux and Meier (1995) noted, in order to enhance self-efficacy, the focus needs to be on painting a picture—making success seem like the most likely outcome. In other words, it's seeing yourself at the finish line and believing that you can get there.

Efficacy is an important aspect of learning, both academically and socially. In this module, you will learn

- About your locus of control and sense of efficacy
- How to develop students' efficacy
- The ways in which collective efficacy benefits students and your colleagues

FIGURE 5.1 FOUR DIMENSIONS OF EFFICACY

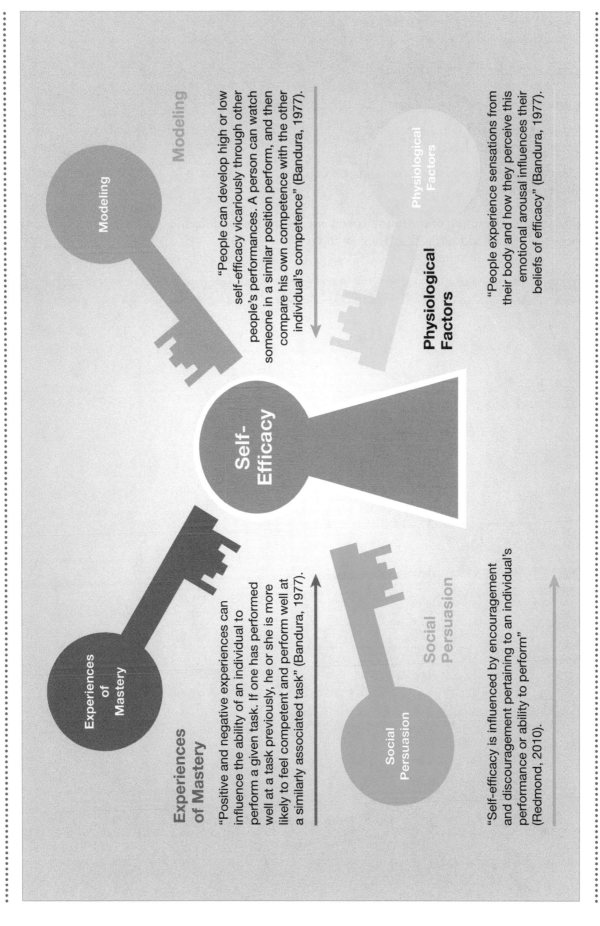

Modeling

"People can develop high or low self-efficacy vicariously through other people's performances. A person can watch someone in a similar position perform, and then compare his own competence with the other individual's competence" (Bandura, 1977).

Physiological Factors

"People experience sensations from their body and how they perceive this emotional arousal influences their beliefs of efficacy" (Bandura, 1977).

Experiences of Mastery

"Positive and negative experiences can influence the ability of an individual to perform a given task. If one has performed well at a task previously, he or she is more likely to feel competent and perform well at a similarly associated task" (Bandura, 1977).

Social Persuasion

"Self-efficacy is influenced by encouragement and discouragement pertaining to an individual's performance or ability to perform" (Redmond, 2010).

SOURCE: Adapted from Penn State Wiki Spaces (n.d.).

VOCABULARY SELF-AWARENESS

Directions: Consider the terms below.

- If it is new to you, write the date in the Level 1 column.
- If you have heard the word before but are not sure that you can use it in a sentence or define it, write the date in the Level 2 column.
- If this word is very familiar to you and you can define it and use it in a sentence, write the date in the Level 3 column.

Update your understanding of the terms as you engage in this module and in your work. Note that there are spaces for you to add terms that are new to you.

WORD	LEVEL 1	LEVEL 2	LEVEL 3	SENTENCE	DEFINITION
Efficacy					
Locus of control					
Mastery experiences					
Imaginal experiences					
Confidence					
Help-seeking					
Learning pit					

WORD	LEVEL 1	LEVEL 2	LEVEL 3	SENTENCE	DEFINITION
Self-assessment					
Collective efficacy					
Safe practice					

Level 1 = This word is new to me.

Level 2 = I have heard this word before.

Level 3 = I know the definition and I can use it in a sentence!

CASEL Connections for educators, students, and schools in this module:

SELF-AWARENESS	SELF-MANAGEMENT	SOCIAL AWARENESS	RELATIONSHIP SKILLS	RESPONSIBLE DECISION MAKING
Self-efficacy	Locus of control		Collective efficacy	Collective efficacy
Mastery experiences	Self-efficacy			Safe practice
Confidence	Goal setting			
Learning pit				

EFFICACY BEGINS WITH SELF

Do you believe in your ability to accomplish your professional goals? In other words, do you have a strong sense of efficacy? Pandemic teaching, and the return to in-person learning with the associated challenges of students who may be less engaged and who may be absent a lot, has challenged our beliefs in our ability to accomplish great things with students.

> *Do you believe in your ability to accomplish your professional goals?*

As Tschannen-Moran and Woolfolk Hoy (2001) noted, efficacy beliefs impact educators' persistence when things do not go as planned and their ability to support students who struggle with learning. Teachers with a stronger sense of efficacy

- Tend to exhibit greater levels of planning and organization

- Are more open to new ideas and are more willing to experiment with new methods to better meet the needs of their students

- Are more persistent and resilient when things do not go smoothly

- Are less critical of students when they make errors

- Are less inclined to refer a difficult student to special education (Protheroe, 2008, p. 43)

There is also evidence that low teacher efficacy is related to teacher burnout and teacher turnover. As Zhu et al. (2018) noted, teacher efficacy impacted several burnout dimensions, including emotional exhaustion, depersonalization, and a reduced sense of personal accomplishment. One of the ways that educators can take care of themselves is to monitor their sense of efficacy and act on areas that are impacting their effectiveness.

NOTE TO SELF

You can learn about your efficacy, at least as it relates to school. Respond to the questions on the Teachers' Sense of Efficacy Scale.

Directions: Please indicate your opinion about each of the questions in the following chart by marking any one of the nine responses in the columns on the right side, ranging from (1) "None at all" to (9) "A great deal" as each represents a degree on the continuum.

Please respond to each of the questions by considering the combination of your *current* ability, resources, and opportunity to do each of the following in your present position.	None to all		Very little		Some degree		Quite a bit		A great deal
1. How much can you do to control disruptive behavior in the classroom?	①	②	③	④	⑤	⑥	⑦	⑧	⑨
2. How much can you do to motivate students who show low interest in school work?	①	②	③	④	⑤	⑥	⑦	⑧	⑨
3. How much can you do to calm a student who is disruptive or noisy?	①	②	③	④	⑤	⑥	⑦	⑧	⑨
4. How much can you do to help your students value learning?	①	②	③	④	⑤	⑥	⑦	⑧	⑨
5. To what extent can you craft good questions for your students?	①	②	③	④	⑤	⑥	⑦	⑧	⑨
6. How much can you do to get children to follow classroom rules?	①	②	③	④	⑤	⑥	⑦	⑧	⑨
7. How much can you do to get students to believe they can do well in school work?	①	②	③	④	⑤	⑥	⑦	⑧	⑨
8. How well can you establish a classroom management system with each group of students?	①	②	③	④	⑤	⑥	⑦	⑧	⑨
9. To what extent can you use a variety of assessment strategies?	①	②	③	④	⑤	⑥	⑦	⑧	⑨
10. To what extent can you provide an alternative explanation or example when students are confused?	①	②	③	④	⑤	⑥	⑦	⑧	⑨
11. How much can you assist families in helping their children do well in school?	①	②	③	④	⑤	⑥	⑦	⑧	⑨
12. How well can you implement alternative teaching strategies in your classroom?	①	②	③	④	⑤	⑥	⑦	⑧	⑨

SOURCE: Tschannen-Moran and Hoy (n.d.).

(Continued)

(Continued)

Now, use the following to find your averages:

Average for the Entire Teachers' Sense of Efficacy Scale (Add all the numbers you have circled and divide by 12.)	
Efficacy in Student Engagement (Add the numbers you circled for items 2, 4, 7, and 11 and then divide by 4.)	
Efficacy in Instructional Strategies (Add the numbers you circled for items 5, 9, 10, and 12 and then divide by 4.)	
Efficacy in Classroom Management (Add the numbers you circled for items 1, 3, 6, and 8 and then divide by 4.)	

If you want to compare yourself with a national sample, here are the averages (and remember, these are pre-pandemic numbers).

- Total Scaled = 7.1

- Efficacy in Student Engagement = 7.2

- Efficacy in Instructional Strategies = 7.3

- Efficacy in Classroom Management = 6.7

Now, spend some time analyzing your efficacy:

Which is my strongest area?	_____ Efficacy in Student Engagement _____ Efficacy in Instructional Strategies _____ Efficacy in Classroom Management
Which area would I most like to focus on?	_____ Efficacy in Student Engagement _____ Efficacy in Instructional Strategies _____ Efficacy in Classroom Management
What is my plan to develop my efficacy in this area?	

Former superintendent David Lorden identified several behaviors associated with a strong sense of efficacy. Consider the actions you might take to build, or rebuild, your efficacy.

ASPECT	APPROACH	ACTIONS TO TAKE
Difficult tasks	See tasks as challenges to be mastered; sees tasks as deeply interesting; is engrossed in tasks	
Goals	Sets challenging goals and is strongly committed to them	
Persistence and effort	Struggles through tasks; exerts great effort; sustains effort in the face of failure	
Failure and setbacks	Attributes failure to insufficient effort or knowledge or skills that are acquirable; recovers quickly from setbacks	
Outlook	Positive and understands that efforts will make a difference	

CASE IN POINT

Winter break has finally arrived, and Trisha Morgia has been doing some personal reflection and goal setting for the back half of the school year. She has been frustrated with the mornings in her classroom. She often uses the copy machine before school, but it easily jams, which can put her behind schedule. Once the students arrive, she feels like she is constantly reminding them to put away their supplies from their backpacks, nagging them to begin their morning work, and putting out emotional fires that seem to spring up from things that happen before her students even enter her room. It leaves her feeling frazzled and exhausted before the first hour of school is even finished.

She identifies three main challenges with the morning:

1. She feels stressed when the copy machine sets her behind.

(Continued)

(Continued)

2. Her students don't have a way to stay organized that helps them know whether they've completed everything that has to get done when they arrive in class.

3. She has to prompt students so often with their morning tasks she doesn't have enough time to fully support students who need an emotional check-in in the morning, so she is often reactive instead of proactive.

Then she sets goals to help her address the challenges.

Her first goal is to get any photocopying for the next day completed after school so that she doesn't have to visit the machine in the morning. Instead, she decides to replace the time she would have spent at the copy machine to get her ready for the day, doing a breathing exercise or guided meditation in her classroom.

Her second goal is to teach her students how to use a morning checklist that lists all the items they should accomplish each morning. She hopes that this will help them build independence and accountability.

Her third goal is to incorporate a pocket chart feelings thermometer that students respond to as soon as they enter the classroom. She intends to use this to be proactive and, during morning work time, to check in with students who identify that they are feeling certain emotions. Armed with these new goals and intentions, she is excited to get back to the classroom in January.

> **How do you think Ms. Morgia's goals addressed the challenges she identified in her classroom? Would you have set different goals? If yes, what would those be?**

EFFICACY CONTINUES WITH STUDENTS

As we noted in the "Building Background" section of this module, efficacy requires that we work toward the desired result. Thus, the starting point for students is goal setting. Remember, when students understand the goal and commit to it, they learn a lot more. The goals they have may be academic and social or emotional. The three clarity questions we developed are the starting place for student efficacy. For each lesson, students should be able to answer these questions:

> When students understand the goal and commit to it, they learn a lot more.

- What am I learning today?
- Why am I learning this?
- How will I know that I learned it?

The first question focuses on the intended learning for the lesson. For example, *I am learning about the life cycles of plants.* Or *I am learning to actively listen to my partner.* These learning intentions need to be discussed and understood if they are going to make a difference in terms of student efficacy. When a student says, "I don't want to learn about plants" or "I can't do this," their efficacy is tested.

The second question focuses on relevance. When students understand the importance or usefulness of what they are learning, they are much more likely to engage in self-regulation. And when they see the relevance in their learning, they are much more likely to be motivated to learn. When we fail to explain the relevance of the learning to students, they may not choose to mobilize resources and focus on learning. Again, this results in reduced efficacy.

The final question focuses on what it means to learn something, or what success in learning looks like. It's not how you, the teacher, will know they learned it. That's important, but student efficacy is built *when they know how they will know that they have learned.* This may be the most important aspect of developing student efficacy. When students understand what success looks like, they are much more likely to commit to the goal. Think about your own experiences. If you have a task to do and success is not defined, how do you respond? Are you less likely to engage fully in the task? Are you more likely to give up if you face barriers? The same is true for students. When they are not sure what success looks like, fear creeps into the lesson and they worry about how they will be judged.

We cannot emphasize this enough. When students do not know what they are learning, why they are learning something, or what success looks like, their willingness to muster their resources and allocate effort is reduced. When students have repeated experiences in which they do not achieve the desired result, their efficacy is compromised, and they start to believe that they are destined to fail.

Imagine, instead, a classroom in which students co-construct the criteria for success. The teacher may share the expected learning intentions and then engage students in a discussion about why this might be important and how they will know that they learned it. We do not mean to imply that teachers simply tell students the answers to the three clarity questions every lesson, but rather that there are many ways to build student efficacy through discussions about these questions.

As an example, a kindergarten class was reading the book *Enemy Pie* (2000). When asked why, Jordan said, "We're learning to be nice. And what it means to be nice." When asked why, Jordan responded, "Well, we are not always nice on the playground. And we need to learn how to be nice so that we can keep friends."

When asked how they would know they learned it, Jordan answered, "When I wake up and I am not mad at anyone."

Interestingly, no other student in the class responded to the *how* question that way, but rather, they had their own ways of knowing how they would know that they learned to be nicer to their peers.

NOTE TO SELF

Consider an upcoming lesson. What do you want students to learn and why? How will you know they learned it? And how will you communicate this to students?

What do I want students to learn?	
Why is this relevant or important to them?	
How will they know they learned it?	
How will I communicate these aspects to students?	

BUILDING CONFIDENCE

It's important that students maintain a "just right" level of *confidence*. Low levels of confidence compromise efficacy as students will not put forth the effort and thus are unlikely to see the results. When students are over-confident, they are less likely to focus on the learning, believing that they have already learned what they need to know. Confidence can be enhanced

- When credible and trustworthy people (e.g., teachers, parents, peers) attribute success to the student

- When a student observes another person complete the task and comes to see that they are capable of the same

- When students feel excitement and satisfaction from the learning experience and mastering the learning

- Where challenging expectations are realized (but less so when non-challenging expectations are met)

- When social persuasion of others helps nudge students toward mastery

- When it is "normal here" to invest, learn from failures and errors, and others are seen to be having similar pathways of success and failure leading to mastery (Hattie et al., 2021)

A quick review of approaches to building confidence can be found in Figure 5.2. Note that several of these have been addressed in this module or other modules. We share this so that you have information about confidence building with students in one place.

FIGURE 5.2 WAYS TO BUILD STUDENT CONFIDENCE

APPROACH	EXPLANATION
Set goals together	One of the most effective ways of building student confidence is making sure everyone is on the same page about learning goals. There is value in having clear learning intentions and success criteria. To build confidence, students and tutors need to understand and agree upon the goals for learning.
Encourage self-assessment	Providing students opportunities to improve learning by encouraging ownership of it is a huge step toward building student confidence. When students learn to self-assess, the role of the teacher becomes to validate and challenge rather than to decide if students have learned. When we do this, student understanding, ownership, enthusiasm for learning, and, of course, confidence increase.
Give useful feedback	Feedback should make someone feel good about where they are and get them excited about where they can go. This is the exact mindset that develops as we continue building our learners' confidence in the classroom.

(Continued)

(Continued)

APPROACH	EXPLANATION
Empty their heads	Students tend to lose confidence in themselves because they feel they're struggling more than they are. Every once in a while, we've got to get learners to unpack everything in their heads through review and open discussion to show them just how much they've accomplished.
Show that effort is normal	Nothing kills confidence more than for a student to think they're the only one in class that doesn't understand something. Focus on the effort that everyone is making. A good way of building student confidence in such a case is by having that struggling student pair up with one of the others who has aced the topic and get them to explain it.
Celebrate success	Any kind of success in learning, no matter how big or small, deserves to be acknowledged and celebrated. This might mean more to some students than to others, but it's still a great way of building student confidence.

SOURCE: Adapted from Crockett (2019).

HELP-SEEKING

Help-seeking is a crucial skill in learning and is considered an example of self-regulation in learning. The ability to seek help first requires that the student recognize that they have reached an impasse. For instance, a student who has been working on a complex math problem realizes that they have tried everything that they can think of but are now stuck. Another dimension of help-seeking is the social environment. That same student considers the social context and makes a decision about whether it is psychologically safe to do so. If the student thinks that asking for help will either threaten their social standing (e.g., "My classmates will think I'm dumb") or their reputation with the adult (e.g., "My teacher will think I'm dumb") then they might choose to go it alone or give up. Their goals may also factor into whether they seek help or not. Chou and Chang (2021) describe help-seekers across three categories:

> Help-seeking is associated with higher levels of achievement (Ryan et al., 2005) but is negatively impacted by stereotype threat.

- **Strategic help-seekers** seek help for learning, as their goals are primarily mastery-driven ("I need help and I want to learn this.")

- **Executive help-seekers** are looking for help to complete the task, as their goals are primarily performance-driven ("I need help because I want to get a better grade than my classmates.")

- **Avoidant help-seekers** perceive that asking for help is a threat and a sign of failure ("I don't want anyone to think I can't do this.")

Help-seeking is associated with higher levels of achievement (Ryan et al., 2005) but is negatively impacted by stereotype threat. A review of academic help-seeking in African American students found that some believed that help was not readily available to them or that it reflected negatively on them, approached peers more frequently than teachers, and were more likely to hide their need for help (Davis-Bowman, 2021).

Help-seeking for the purposes of learning declines among all students as they move through their educational careers. Ryan and Shin (2011) learned that as students got older, they asked peers more often for help, but mostly for expediency rather than learning, such as asking to copy an answer. They too found that there was a social component to even this kind of help-seeking. The sixth graders in their study weighed the social environment, especially their standing with peers. These students reported that asking a peer who was more popular than them, or who was a high-achieving student, was too socially risky.

NOTE TO SELF

Consider ways that you can create a help-seeking culture in your classroom, especially one that is focused on learning rather than on performance. Use the chart below to identify ways you are currently promoting help-seeking and techniques you can use to grow them.

PROMOTE HELP-SEEKING AMONG PEERS	
Use peer tutoring in the class.	
Provide times for students to check in with one another about a skill or concept.	
Create student study groups and "study buddies."	

(Continued)

(Continued)

PROMOTE HELP-SEEKING FROM YOU	
Model how you seek help in your life.	
Pause frequently throughout lessons to invite questions.	
Specify resources that they can turn to for help (teacher, peers, textbooks, online resources).	
Reinforce that help-seeking for learning is valued.	
Watch for nonverbal signs that a student needs help (facial expression, body language).	
Offer help discreetly and proactively (e.g., "How can I help? I have the time").	

THE LEARNING PIT

The idea of the *learning pit* was introduced by Nottingham (2007) who noted that students needed to be challenged and they needed experiences in which they overcome challenges. The model proposed by Nottingham has four phases that comprise the learning challenge:

- **Concept:** The content that students are familiar with but have yet to master.

- **Conflict:** An intentional cognitive conflict that will allow students to engage in productive struggle.

- **Construct:** Students use skills, tools, and methods to overcome the challenge. Often, this involves collaborating with others to find new clarity.

- **Consider:** Students reflect on their learning journey and consider new ways to use the information they've acquired.

> *Students need to recognize the need for help and have the skills to seek out that help.*

To build efficacy, students need to have worthy goals, which we have already addressed. They also need to recognize the need for help and have the skills to seek out that help, which we have also already addressed. But to struggle through a learning task requires they develop increased perseverance. When teachers specifically and intentionally tell students that learning involves struggle and that we can expect to be in the learning pit often, they grant permission for students to grapple with ideas and not give up. In other words, classrooms need a norm that clearly communicates that errors are expected and celebrated. Figure 5.3 contains a visual of the learning pit inspired by Nottingham.

Our point here is that at the bottom of the pit, efficacy is tested. When students are not sure what to do to accomplish the learning goal, they may retreat and agree that it's too hard or not possible to accomplish the challenge. When that happens, their efficacy is tested and may be compromised. When they start to figure things out and begin the climb out of the pit, their efficacy is developed and reinforced. When students regularly experience appropriate struggle and subsequent success, they become increasingly efficacious. And there is evidence that efficacy in one area transfers to others (Massar & Malmberg, 2017).

FIGURE 5.3 THE LEARNING PIT

SOURCE: Nottingham (2017).

The learning pit is one way to develop students' efficacy. How might you ensure that students know that productive struggle is valued in your class and that mistakes are welcomed?

What are your thoughts and plans for encouraging struggle and valuing mistakes?

SELF-ASSESSMENT

As we noted earlier, *self-assessment* can build students' confidence. But more than that, self-assessments allow students to build their efficacy. Efficacy is fed by evidence, and some of the evidence students accept comes from adults and peers. But it's very powerful when students learn to self-assess and monitor their own progress. They see more clearly and directly that their efforts have an impact; that they are a deciding factor in the outcome.

> There is evidence that efficacy in one area transfers to others.

Self-assessment is the metacognitive process whereby a student examines their work or abilities (Brown & Harris, 2014). Brown and Harris call this a "core competency" for fostering the necessary self-regulation skills that accelerate student learning (p. 27). Placing students in the active role of determining whether they have learned something, and how they might adjust their deployment of strategies to shape their own learning, builds self-regulation. In fact, the ability to self-regulate requires self-assessment (Zimmerman & Moylan, 2009).

Panadero et al. (2017) conducted four meta-analyses on the impact of self-assessment on self-regulation and self-efficacy. They reported that academic self-assessments had a small to medium effect size on self-regulation in three meta-analyses ($d = 0.23$ to 0.65). Their fourth meta-analysis on self-efficacy was even stronger, at $d = 0.73$. In other words, self-assessment is a building block of self-efficacy.

As an example, single-point rubrics can be used for self-assessment. Popularized by the Cult of Pedagogy (Gonzalez, 2014), single-point rubrics contain a list of performance or learning expectations. Unlike analytic rubrics, single-point rubrics only describe the criteria for proficiency rather than all the ways that students could miss the mark or exceed expectations. Originally, educators used these to provide students feedback that they could more easily understand given that there was a lot less language on the tool. During pandemic teaching, educators realized that students could use these tools to determine where they needed additional learning versus where they had reached or exceeded expectations. Of course, students must understand the language on the tool to use it to monitor progress and assess their learning.

For example, fourth graders were asked to retell content that they had read, recording their retellings on video for submission to their teacher. Students were provided the following single-point rubric. Note that students were asked to identify opportunities to *grow* and where they *glow*.

	GROWS	SUCCESS CRITERIA	GLOWS
Main ideas		I tell about the main ideas. I give examples of them.	
Supporting details		My details are linked to the main ideas.	
Sequence		I retell information in the same order as the author.	
Accuracy		I use accurate facts.	

Madlyn, a student in the class, recorded her retelling of *Henry's Freedom Box* (Levine, 2007). After listening to her own retelling, Madlyn completed the self-assessment, noting *glows* on main ideas and details as well as accuracy. She noted *grow* opportunities in the other categories. She wrote herself a note about details, indicating that she should have provided more specifics. She also noted that she told some of the events out of order, but wanted to know if that was really important. Her teacher reviewed Madlyn's self-assessment and agreed with her *glow* areas. The teacher also scheduled a time to talk with Madlyn about sequence.

> *It's very powerful when students learn to self-assess and monitor their own progress.*

During their conference, Madlyn said, "I didn't tell the whole thing in order, but I think it was still good. Does it only have to be in the order of the book?"

The teacher noted that there are good reasons to describe events out of sequence, especially when you have a theme. As the teacher said, "If you focus on the theme, which we will be starting next week, then you can talk about different parts of the book that support the theme."

NOTE TO SELF

Self-assessment is a powerful tool teachers can use to foster student efficacy. Students learn to self-assess through a series of experiences. Consider the following three ways that students learn to assess their own work and develop plans for using them (Minero, 2016).

TOPIC	DEFINITION	HOW I CAN USE IT
Seeing examples of mastery	To know what is expected, or what success looks like, students need exemplars and examples	
Learning vocabulary	To be able to judge process and mastery, students need to use the correct terminology; the words they use represent the concepts they have	
Practicing peer critique	Providing feedback to peers allows students to analyze more examples and become increasingly comfortable receiving feedback and recognizing their own level of performance	

CASE IN POINT

René Hamm had noticed that the students in his U.S. History classes seemed bored with their typical daily routine, which included lecture, note-taking, discussion, and reading texts and primary sources. He decided to incorporate more collaborative, small-group opportunities into his instruction, but even though his students are eleventh graders, he knows it is important to make sure that they understand how to interact appropriately and effectively, especially since this is something new in his class.

At the start of the unit about the Great Depression, he decided to take one class period to explain the new types of projects the students would encounter during the unit and work with them to set both behavior and academic goals. The students were very excited to change things up in class and were eager to share ideas for goals that would hold them accountable both academically and behaviorally. In addition, the students decided to self-evaluate their progress toward their goals at the end of each week using a Likert scale for each goal. Mr. Hamm was genuinely encouraged by his students' responses and was just as eager as they were to start the unit.

Throughout the unit, there were definitely class periods that went more smoothly than others, but overall, the students worked hard to accomplish their goals each week. Occasionally, Mr. Hamm had to work with the students to adjust goals by adding to them or making them more specific. At the end of the unit, the students felt a greater sense of accomplishment and a deeper understanding of the academic content as a result of the new opportunities for learning as well as of the accountability set forth by their goals. Mr. Hamm also agreed to continue this type of instruction for the next unit.

> **How did involving the students in setting their own goals for academic and behavioral expectations help develop their individual and collective efficacy?**

COLLECTIVE EFFICACY IS NURTURED BY SCHOOLS

Thus far, we have focused on self-efficacy, but Bandura expanded the notion and noted that there was also an impact of collective efficacy. The concept of *collective efficacy* was introduced by Bandura (1997), who defined it as "a group's shared belief in the conjoint capabilities to organize and execute the courses of action required to produce given levels of attainment" (p. 447). That's pretty technical, so we will take it apart. It is a group of people. And this group believes in the abilities of their group. And this group does what it takes to achieve their goal. Collective efficacy has been studied rather extensively in education and there is strong evidence of the impact on students' learning (Ells, 2011).

In addition, as Hoy et al. (2002) note, there is a reciprocal relationship between individual and collective efficacy. As one gets stronger, so does the other. Strong collective efficacy seems to encourage individual teachers to make more effective use of the skills they already have. And strong individual efficacy allows teams to function more productively. In terms of educators, collective teacher efficacy is super powerful, with an effect size of 1.36, meaning it has the potential to significantly accelerate learning.

Collective responsibility, as will be discussed further in Module 6, is foundational for collective efficacy to thrive. If a group does not believe that it is their responsibility to move learning forward, student achievement suffers. In schools where there is a high degree of collective responsibility for academic success and failure, students thrive. While collective responsibility is important, it is not sufficient. Without action, collective responsibility devolves into collective guilt. Collective efficacy requires actions that are purposeful and designed to yield results. Keep this in mind: collective teacher efficacy, with an effect size of 1.36, is nearly three times as influential as socioeconomic status (0.52) on student achievement. Teams that enjoy a high degree of collective efficacy set goals for themselves, pursue them, gauge their progress, make changes as needed, and evaluate their impact. When highly efficacious teams proliferate across a school, the organization becomes efficacious.

> *Collective efficacy requires actions that are purposeful and designed to yield results.*

To our thinking, there are two major parts to this idea. First, impact is realized when a group of educators have systems for determining what students need to learn, have concrete plans to ensure that learning, and measure their impact, making adjustments when students do not learn as expected. Second, this group of educators believes that their students can learn and that they have the power (skills, knowledge, beliefs) to ensure that students learn. As Bandura (2000) noted, "Unless people believe that they can produce desired effects and forestall undesired ones by their actions, they have little incentive to act" (p. 75). *Mastery experiences* are among the most powerful ways to build collective efficacy (Bandura, 1986). When teachers practice together actions and strategies to promote student learning, they can determine where their strengths and weaknesses lie. This is one of the most powerful sources of efficacy information (Tschannen-Moran et al., 1998). When groups of educators experience success and accomplishment, they begin to attribute those successes to their actions rather than outside forces.

To facilitate mastery experiences, we have developed a collective efficacy learning cycle (see Figure 5.4). Our model starts with a common challenge. The operative word here is *common*, which means that the group agrees on it. And that means that they had an opportunity to talk about it. School leaders should not simply analyze data in their offices and announce goals to teachers. Instead, groups need to grapple with the data and identify goals that will challenge them. There is evidence that groups with a strong sense of collective efficacy set higher goals for themselves (Goddard et al., 2004).

> *Groups with a strong sense of collective efficacy set higher goals for themselves.*

FIGURE 5.4   COLLECTIVE EFFICACY CYCLE

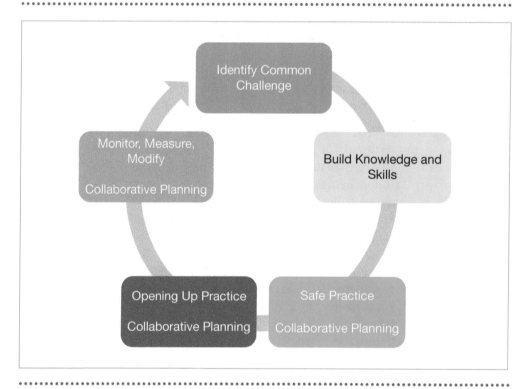

SOURCE: Fisher et al. (2020).

As part of the collective efficacy cycles, teams identify their *common challenge* and what they would like to see as an outcome. From there, teams set forth on a learning journey. Highly efficacious teams understand there is still much to learn but remain open to a variety of learning opportunities. Sometimes, they read books, articles, or websites. Other times, they attend workshops or seminars. The format is less important than the actions that result. What is important is the realization that there is learning that the team can do together.

As they learn, team members engage in what we call *safe practice*. They get to try on ideas and test them out. They get to fail and learn from their mistakes. At this stage, leaders are listening and engaging in discussions with teachers and not simply observing them and giving critical feedback. Teachers are given the opportunity to try out new approaches without the anxiety of having others watch.

Naturally, this will lead to *opening up practice*. Groups with strong collective efficacy do not simply replicate strategies from their peers, but rather deepen their understanding of the nuances of the approaches their peers use. This stage also invites vicarious experiences in which teachers learn from watching each other, noting the impact that the instruction has on student learning. Vicarious experiences are an additional way that collective efficacy can be built (Bandura, 1986). Peer learning during this period of safe practice builds the belief systems of the team that they can accomplish their goals.

When practice becomes more public, the effect of modeling is mobilized. Modeling and social persuasion are also valuable in creating and maintaining collective efficacy, even if they are not as powerful as mastery experiences (Bandura, 1986).

And, perhaps most importantly, highly efficacious groups *monitor, measure, and modify*. They track successes and note their impact. This information feeds the group as they continue their efforts. The group begins to see their efforts, rather than outside factors, as the source of impact. That is not to say that everything a group with high collective efficacy tries works the first time. The difference is that they *monitor, measure, and modify* their efforts to achieve the common challenge. And they attribute the success they experience to their efforts and set new goals the next time they begin the cycle.

NOTE TO SELF

Collective efficacy cycles require planning. To build the collective power of your team, plan a 10-week cycle in which you decide on a goal. The goal should be worthwhile and challenging, but achievable. Remember that it takes several rounds to build collective efficacy, increasing expectations following each success. From there, identify the new learning that will occur. How many weeks will you devote to that? Also, plan time for safe practice and opening up practice. Then identify the data you will collect to monitor impact. And don't forget to plan a celebration and then identify the next goal.

(Continued)

(Continued)

Targeted Instructional Area: _____

Common Challenge:

CYCLE # DATE SPAN:	INPUT New learning for teachers	SAFE PRACTICE Teachers experiment with the new practice in a low-risk environment	OPENING UP CLASSROOM PRACTICE Teachers observe each other and engage in structured reflection/ feedback	MONITOR MEASURE MODIFY Collect information on impact, make revisions, celebrate, and establish new goals
Week 1				
Week 2				
Week 3				
Week 4				
Week 5				
Week 6				
Week 7				
Week 8				
Week 9				
Week 10				

SOURCE: Adapted from Chula Vista Elementary School District (2018).

CASE IN POINT

Delores Blackburn is the principal at Pinewood Elementary School. The school has performed below the state average in both math and literacy for the past three years, so the school improvement plan has reflected a focus in both areas. In the past two years, the school has emphasized high-quality literacy instruction, and the teachers have worked hard to incorporate small-group instruction, vocabulary, and word work as well as a range of reading material. They even secured a grant to help send books home with the students in an effort to build their home libraries.

The results from the end-of-year assessment data were released, and Ms. Blackburn was thrilled to see a huge improvement in the average literacy scores. The teachers and students had worked hard, and the results showed. Unfortunately, the average math scores had dropped even lower than the previous year. Determined to help teachers make improvements in math instruction throughout the building, but without much input from the staff, Ms. Blackburn goes to work outlining the expectations for math instruction for the following school year.

At the last staff meeting before the summer, the staff throws a party to celebrate the gains shown in the school's literacy scores. Everyone is feeling great. Eager to continue that momentum and excitement in the following year, Ms. Blackburn announces the new expectations for math instruction and encourages the staff to think over the summer about how they would meet those goals. Although it was not her intention, the staff leaves the meeting feeling deflated, confused, and without real direction.

> **How could Ms. Blackburn have handled this situation differently to build her staff's individual and collective efficacy?**

SELF-ASSESSMENT

The continued development of our self-efficacy and collective efficacy requires that we revisit our own goals periodically. Revisit the major concepts and practices profiled in this module and use the traffic light scale to determine where you are now in each practice.

Menu of Practices on Individual and Collective Efficacy

Use the traffic light scale to reflect on your current practices as they relate to efficacy at the levels of self, students, and school. What areas do you want to strengthen?

INDIVIDUAL OPPORTUNITIES	
I am able to examine my sense of efficacy as an educator.	
I am able to identify areas of strength and places to grow my efficacy as an educator.	
STUDENT-LEVEL OPPORTUNITIES	
I teach using principles of clarity to build student efficacy.	
I use techniques to foster "just right" levels of confidence among my students.	
I invest in productive student help-seeking behaviors among peers and of me.	
I use techniques to build persistence among students.	
Students in my class regularly self-assess in order to measure progress toward goals.	
SCHOOL-LEVEL APPROACHES	
I personally contribute to the collective efficacy of my team at school.	
We use a cycle of inquiry to drive our team's work.	

What do I need to do to change my reds to yellows?

Who can support me to turn my yellows into greens?

How am I using my greens to positively contribute to the good of the whole?

Access resources, tools, and guides for this module at
resources.corwin.com/theselplaybook

MODULE 6

....

COMMUNITY OF CARE

BUILDING BACKGROUND

Well-being is an important part of the social-emotional learning that humans need to acquire. The dictionary defines well-being as "the state of being comfortable, healthy, or happy." And that's a good place to start, but it seems that well-being is bigger than that. You and your students may ask yourselves how satisfied you are with your whole life, which includes both personal and professional aspects. As educators, perhaps we should start saying life-work balance, rather than always putting work first.

Well-being also includes a sense of purpose. When we are needed, when we have a mission to accomplish, when we see the impact of our efforts, our overall well-being is stronger. And when we are in control, our well-being is stronger. That does not mean that we have to make all the decisions. In fact, there are decisions that others make for us. But when we know that we can control some aspects of our lives, we feel better. The New Economics Foundation (2012) described well-being as the following:

> Well-being can be understood as how people feel and how they function, both on a personal and a social level, and how they evaluate their lives as a whole.

Most people agree that this is a desirable state. And we strive for well-being in our lives and in the lives of our students and colleagues. That has been translated into "take care of yourself." And we believe that people should be encouraged to take care of themselves. In fact, some people need permission to take care of themselves, as they have been socialized to believe that taking care of themselves is selfish. As we will explore, there are a number of things that humans can choose to do that improve their overall health and well-being.

But we offer a caution here. Educators are busy and some note that they do not have time to take care of themselves. They then feel guilty, increasing the pressure that they experience, which decreases their overall sense of well-being. And some are even blamed for not taking care of themselves. When they fail to exercise or sleep well or whatever, it becomes a situation in which the victim is blamed. Over time, when our well-being is compromised, we burn out and quit our jobs. We do so in protection of ourselves. An educator told us that she was having suicidal thoughts daily because she did not feel effective in her role. She quit the profession to protect herself, but some of her colleagues said that she should have taken better care of herself.

> Self-care isn't enough; we need community care to thrive.

As Dockray (2019) noted, self-care isn't enough. The mantra "If *you* want to feel better, *you* need to do the labor yourself, for yourself" is in need of being to be updated because we need community care to thrive. Nakita Valerio suggested that we engage in community care, which she defined for *Mashable* as: "People committed to leveraging their privilege to be there for one another in various ways." Valerio compares a community of care to an extended family in which individuals routinely perform acts of kindness and compassion for one another.

That's why we titled this final module "Community of Care." We need to take care of others. We have a moral responsibility to our colleagues. Some will argue that they do not have time to care for others; that they are up to their ears in work and personal issues. But if we each could contribute to the well-being of others, we might just make our personal and professional lives better. And remember, building a community of care means that others are helping you to take care of yourself, especially when times are difficult for you. It's a collective responsibility and one that has the potential to provide a protective factor for us, our students, and our schools.

As Katherine Center, named "the queen of comfort reads" by BookPage, says:

> We are at our finest when we take care of each other.

What does that mean to you? What are the implications of this for educators? For us, it means that we work to take care of ourselves, each other, and our community. In doing so, we do not compromise our well-being but rather contribute to, and benefit from, the community.

In this module, we will explore how to

- Take care of yourself

- Teach students about self-care and well-being

- Create a community of care in your school

VOCABULARY SELF-AWARENESS

Directions: Consider the terms below.

- If it is new to you, write the date in the Level 1 column.

- If you have heard the word before but are not sure that you can use it in a sentence or define it, write the date in the Level 2 column.

- If this word is very familiar to you and you can define it and use it in a sentence, write the date in the Level 3 column.

Update your understanding of the terms as you engage in this module and in your work. Note that there are spaces for you to add terms that are new to you.

WORD	LEVEL 1	LEVEL 2	LEVEL 3	SENTENCE	DEFINITION
Physical activity					
Emotional well-being					
Meta-analysis					
Mindfulness					
School climate					

WORD	LEVEL 1	LEVEL 2	LEVEL 3	SENTENCE	DEFINITION
Communication competency					
Collective responsibility					

Level 1 = This word is new to me.

Level 2 = I have heard this word before.

Level 3 = I know the definition and I can use it in a sentence!

CASEL Connections for educators, students, and schools in this module:

SELF-AWARENESS	SELF-MANAGEMENT	SOCIAL AWARENESS	RELATIONSHIP SKILLS	RESPONSIBLE DECISION MAKING
Mindfulness	Physical wellness Emotional well-being	Reaching out to others experiencing difficulty Trauma-sensitive design	School climate Communication competency	Collective responsibility

A COMMUNITY OF CARE BEGINS WITH SELF

It has often been noted that you can't pour from an empty cup. Without individuals who are socially and emotionally strong, there is little possibility that they will have much in their reservoir to invest in others. Building a community of care in the classroom and school requires that its members are physically and emotionally healthy. Further, when one's well-being is compromised, they have the tools internally and externally to regain their footing.

> A community of care requires that members shepherd the welfare of others.

As we have noted, a community of care requires that members shepherd the welfare of others. A community of care doesn't emerge simply because all its members are invested in their own well-being. However, when members of an organization do not do so, a community of care cannot form. Taking care of oneself is foundational.

INVEST IN YOUR EMOTIONAL WELL-BEING

Biological factors interact with social and emotional factors in ways that are increasingly understood as affecting one another. A definition of the mind-body connection is that the thoughts, emotions, and dispositions we possess can positively or negatively impact our physical well-being.

Negative manifestation of emotions can be a contributing factor to high blood pressure, susceptibility to illness, and chronic pain. Bessel van der Kolk's (2015) book, *The Body Keeps the Score,* has remained on the bestsellers list since its publication in large part because the mind-body connection, while complex, can be positively impacted by intentional actions we can take to bolster our emotional health.

The emotional wellness of the individuals in an organization is crucial for fostering a community of care. The World Health Organization (2004), noting that "there is no health without mental health," calls positive mental health "the foundation for well-being and effective functioning for both the individual and the community" (p. 11). A community of care at the classroom and school levels invests in fostering, maintaining, and strengthening the emotional wellness of its members.

There are a number of actions that people take to maintain and regain emotional wellness. Some find the cathartic effects of journaling rewarding; for another, this might seem more like drudgery. Doug enjoys his hot yoga class while Nancy views it as a form of torture. The point is that what matters most is that the technique you use works for *you*. We in no way present ourselves as mental health experts. Professional counseling and physician-supervised medications may be in order. But having said that, a few ideas are useful for designing your own emotional wellness plan:

- **Keep isolation at bay.** Pay attention to the social connections you enjoy and understand that human interaction is necessary for your emotional health.

- **Set aside time for yourself every day.** Education is such a service-oriented profession and attracts people who see themselves as givers, not takers. But emotional well-being requires investment in self. Bracket your time so that you have time to calm your mind. It's not selfish to devote some time every day to meditate, read, reflect, or enjoy nature.

- **Attend to your community like you would a garden.** Nurture your community of care by investing in the well-being of others. We'll return to this idea in more detail later in this module. However, we boost ourselves when we exhibit caring for others. The thank-you note, the sincere compliment, or the easing of someone else's burden has a positive effect on your emotional health, too.

> *It's not selfish to devote some time every day to meditate, read, reflect, or enjoy nature.*

- **Check in regularly with your own emotions.** Emotional wellness is not static; it is regularly buffeted by positive and negative circumstances that occur in our personal and professional lives. This is precisely why the developers of the Warwick-Edinburgh Mental Well-Being Scale (WEMWBS), a 14-item self-assessment, invite participants to consider their emotional wellness over a two-week period. The WEMWBS can be found at https://bit.ly/WEMWBS_14, and we encourage you to use it regularly to gauge how your emotional experiences are manifesting.

REACH OUT TO OTHERS WHO ARE EXPERIENCING DIFFICULTY

The challenges our colleagues are facing weigh on each of us, too. However, it can feel awkward to talk with them about their well-being. Many of us hold some rigid notions of professional lives versus personal ones and are reluctant to cross an unstated boundary. Our own experience with teaching and writing about adult social-emotional learning is that most educators want to turn the discussion back to their students rather than sit with their own feelings. This is a characteristic of our profession—we keep a steady lens on students. But if we don't expand our focus to include colleagues, we condemn people to wrestle with personal challenges in isolation.

We don't expect you to suddenly become a therapist, or worse yet, to start diagnosing others. But your willingness to open a line of communication with a colleague who you believe is struggling may very well be a light for them. Don't be afraid that you might not say the exact right thing. Your demonstration of caring sends a powerful message to them. Having a few statements or questions in mind can open up the conversation. Remember, it is the power of listening that matters more than talking about the solutions.

> *Don't be afraid you might not say the exact right thing; your demonstration of caring sends a powerful message.*

A fundamental aspect of respect and dignity is the ability to listen and communicate that you have listened. It is no different for the many students who want you to listen to them—they want you to listen to how they are thinking about the problem and not have you rush in with the right answer. They know there is a right answer; their concern is that their thinking is not leading to the right answer—and they want you to listen to how they are thinking and processing and then help them work to find the right answers. Elmer (2019) advises that these questions and statements can be especially helpful in guiding your conversation:

- **Do you want to talk about it? I'm here when you're ready.** This is more direct than simply asking, "Are you okay?" which can tempt the stock reply, "I'm fine."

- **What can I do to help today?** Sometimes doing a simple task together, such as giving a hand at organizing your colleague's class library, can serve as a way to establish a safe space for conversation.

  - **How are you managing?** This question allows you to acknowledge a person's struggles without having to list them.

  - **You're not alone. I may not understand exactly how you feel, but you're not alone.** This counters the temptation to turn the spotlight on yourself and your own challenges. When you're reaching out to someone who you suspect needs support, don't try to match their challenges with your own.

- **That sounds like it's really hard. How are you coping?** Your colleague may name something in particular that they are having difficulty working through. Don't tell them what you did in a similar circumstance; just listen.

- **I'm really sorry you're going through this. I'm here for you if you need me.** Keep the line of communication open. It isn't realistic to believe that a single conversation is going to resolve everything for the person. Complex traumas can't be resolved that way. Letting that person know that you are part of their caring network matters.

> *A fundamental aspect of respect and dignity is the ability to listen and communicate that you have listened.*

CASE IN POINT

Seventh-grade teacher Caleb Puckett hasn't felt like himself. He was thrilled to return to face-to-face instruction with his students after a long period of remote learning. But the return has been bumpier than he expected. His students need more academic and emotional support than he anticipated, and the initial excitement of being in the company of others has been tempered by periodic surges in COVID-19 infections. His instructional day now includes a higher churn of students absent due to quarantine rules and the disruptions caused by frustrated students. His colleagues are tired, too, and there is a sense of discouragement pervading the school.

The net effect has taken its toll on Mr. Puckett. Sleep is fitful, and he wakes up nightly with worries about his students and a longing for the weekend to come faster. "I never used to feel that way, but now I just want the week to be over." The mental lethargy that he is experiencing has resulted in less time spent playing basketball with friends, an activity he has enjoyed since childhood. "I'm having a harder time summing up the energy I need for friends, family, and school," he says.

Imagine that Mr. Puckett is a professional colleague of yours. How might you advise him?

A COMMUNITY OF CARE CONTINUES WITH STUDENTS

Students form the center of the hub of schooling and are vital in the development of a community of caring. As with all members of the school community, they are both receivers of and providers for caring. In the same way that physical and emotional well-being are crucial for adults, so it is for young people.

INVEST IN YOUR STUDENTS' PHYSICAL WELL-BEING

Students carry with them a variety of stressors that can compromise their ability to learn. In fact, this entire playbook is built on the assumption that the social-emotional learning of students is directly linked to their academic and psychological health. When educators had to pivot to distance learning in the spring of 2020, many of us witnessed anew the toll that these circumstances took on our students. Duke University's Flexible Teaching Center, which is dedicated to learner-centered principles across platforms—face-to-face, online, or hybrid—reminded instructors of four important points for supporting students' physical and emotional well-being (Duke University, 2022, ¶ 4). As educators, we must

> *Students carry with them a variety of stressors that can compromise their ability to learn.*

1. First and foremost, recognize that each student has a body

2. Understand that at this particular moment, those bodies are incredibly stressed

3. Understand that stressed bodies learn differently/less well/more slowly

4. Take this into consideration [when] designing our classes, our assignments, and our assessment

Understanding the Links Between Physical Wellness and Learning

There is a strong link between students' physical health and their academic learning. The Visible Learning database developed by John Hattie contains extensive research on the deleterious effects of compromised physical health on academic learning. These influences, in particular, exert a large negative impact on learning. At the top of the list are chronic physical illnesses, including diabetes, asthma, and sickle cell anemia. Analysis of more than 1,000 quantitative studies involving a total of 121,100 students reveals an effect size of –0.44, meaning that there is a high potential that a reversal of learning will occur. (Keep in mind that of the 322 influences on student learning, less than 5 percent fall into this harmful impact range.) Similarly, a meta-analysis of the effects of a high-sugar diet on academic learning reported an effect size of –0.16. A third negative factor is lack of sleep as a function of both duration and quality, at –0.02.

Promoting Physical Wellness

Exercise, as a protective factor and as a technique for addressing these concerns, has a modest positive effect at 0.20, meaning that it is likely to have a positive impact on student learning (not to mention a positive impact on overall health). Many of the studies focus on physical education interventions, which remain an important source of *physical activity*. But one *meta-analysis*, which is a quantitative study of studies, is of particular interest in this context (Bedard et al., 2019). The researchers analyzed 25 studies of physically active preschool through middle school classrooms where academic content was taught through physical movement. For example, students used physical movement during vocabulary instruction, such as mimicking flight to learn the term *fly* or doing the number of jumping jacks corresponding to the answer to a problem in mathematics. In addition to academic gains, these studies reported increased time on task and higher levels of enjoyment. You can learn more about these and other influences at https://www.visiblelearn ingmetax.com.

Classrooms can also incorporate physical activity through "brain breaks" that provide students with a quick, structured teacher-led activity such as a series of stretches or a short dance. One high school teacher we know leads their class through a stadium-style "wave" to encourage whole-body movement. Staci Benak, a high school teacher, reviews mathematical concepts such as negative infinity and positive infinity by leading an aerobics activity (complete with 1980s-style sweat-bands) so that students can move their bodies through space to embody these abstract concepts. Teachers of multilingual learners of all ages are quite familiar with Total Physical Response (TPR), which is the practice of linking movement to language to promote listening comprehension (Asher, 1969). The Centers for Disease Control and Prevention (CDC) provides a document of *Strategies for Classroom Physical Activity in Schools* and advises consideration of the following as you look for ways to incorporate physical activity into academics:

- Culture and context of the classroom and school
- Goals of individual classes or courses
- Preferences and comfort level of individual teachers
- Enjoyment level and preferences of students
- Resources, time, and spaces available (CDC, 2018, p. 9)

CASE IN POINT

Physical educator Jia Cheng leads instruction at her small elementary school of 400 students. Like many PE instructors, she is concerned about the CDC's findings that only 43 percent of elementary students nationwide participate in regular physical activity breaks outside of physical education during the school day. "I know how important movement is for learning," said Ms. Cheng. "But it's a challenge to find many classroom teachers who know how important it is." On numerous occasions, she has observed that even though there is

(Continued)

(Continued)

daily recess, a troubling number of students remain sedentary during that time. "You can't count on the fact that just because they're outside, they'll be moving. There's lots of standing around." Then there's the problem of withholding recess for disciplinary purposes, despite recommendations by many organizations that this doesn't happen. "I see two dozen students every day that are sitting in the lunch arbor because they have had recess taken away," she said.

Ms. Cheng is on a district committee dedicated to bringing daily physical activity to more students. What if a similar committee was operating in your district? Use the CDC recommendations to frame your advice to the committee about future professional learning for teachers in the district.

CONSIDERATIONS	YOUR RECOMMENDATIONS
Culture and context of the classroom and school	
Goals of individual classes or courses	
Preferences and comfort level of individual teachers	
Enjoyment level and preferences of students	
Resources, time, and spaces available	

INVEST IN YOUR STUDENTS' EMOTIONAL WELL-BEING

Chances are pretty good that your interest in this playbook stems in large part from your concerns about the emotional health of your students. In fact, if you followed the student strand throughout these modules, that will be precisely what we are discussing. There are many facets to student emotional well-being, so please consider this to be a starting point for continued discussion throughout the modules.

Emotional well-being in children and adolescents comes down to a simple question: Is this young person flourishing or not?

Emotional well-being in children and adolescents comes down to a simple question: *Is this young person flourishing or not?* Children who are flourishing are making gains in their physical, psychological, and academic growth, while those that are not may display an array of worrisome behaviors. Some may lash out at others or withdraw completely. Others may have high levels of anxiety that immobilize them. Some young people may make risky decisions that negatively impact them.

The World Health Organization has developed a validated five-item assessment of emotional well-being for ages 9 and above. First piloted in 1998, the WHO-5 Satisfaction Index, as it is called, has been used across the world and in fields as varied as medicine, psychiatry, and education. Like the WEMWBS profiled earlier in this module, the WHO-5 asks participants to consider their experiences over the previous two weeks, rather than more narrowly at the time of administration.

OVER THE LAST TWO WEEKS . . .	ALL OF THE TIME	MOST OF THE TIME	MORE THAN HALF OF THE TIME	LESS THAN HALF OF THE TIME	SOME OF THE TIME	AT NO TIME
1. I have felt cheerful and in good spirits.						
2. I have felt calm and relaxed.						
3. I have felt active and vigorous.						
4. I woke up feeling fresh and rested.						
5. My daily life has been filled with things that interest me.						

SOURCE: WHO-5 Well-Being Index (1998).

Understanding the Links Between Emotional Well-Being and Learning

As with physical illness, the effects of negative emotions greatly impact the academic learning of students. At the top of the list are these influences that are likely to have a negative impact:

- Anger: –0.82

- Frustration: –0.52

- Anxiety: –0.36

- Depression: –0.29

Each of these negative emotions occurs across a continuum, from fleeting and momentary to clinical and prolonged. Again, it is important to say that the emotional wellness discussed in this playbook is at a more general level. The strategies discussed are not a substitute for the expertise of mental health professionals who treat young people with debilitating forms of these emotions. However, all of us have seen temporary expressions of these feelings in our own students. An argument with a parent the night before, an upsetting conversation with a friend, or the fear of an upcoming test are just a few examples that can trigger emotional turmoil and thus bring learning to a halt.

Promoting Emotional Well-Being

A sense of well-being, which Hattie defines as "how students think and feel about their lives, especially the presence of pleasant and positive affect (e.g., happiness)," is likely to have a positive impact on learning, with an effect size of 0.36 (https://www.visiblelearningmetax.com). Happiness has an even greater impact (0.53), with the potential to accelerate learning.

> *"Rest is not idleness"; brief breaks from cognition are crucial for memory formation, consolidation of concepts, and divergent thinking.*

Classroom-based *mindfulness* practices have emerged over the last decade as a way to allow students to re-center their attention and thinking. Rather than specifically designed to teach academics, these practices are emotional brain breaks. They are brief, structured, and led by the teacher. A concern among some educators is that breaks like this mean that learning is not occurring. But *f*MRI studies of brain activity have shown otherwise. It turns out that "rest is not idleness" and that brief breaks from cognition are crucial for memory formation, consolidation of concepts, and divergent thinking (Immordino-Yang et al., 2012, p. 352).

Mindfulness practices have a modest influence on student learning (0.28) and include activities such as breathing exercises, calming activities to regain focus, and guided imagery. As with physical activity, the true effectiveness is likely to be the temporary interruption of negative emotions. Performed routinely, they can contribute to a young person's ability to engage in self-regulation of one's emotions. Equipping students with a toolkit of simple techniques they can use on their own, at any time, sounds like a good investment.

Practices such as these should not be viewed as a simple cure-all to a complex problem. "The best way to implement mindfulness is in an integrated way with social and emotional learning," said Linda Lantieri, a founding member of the Collaborative for Academic, Social, and Emotional Learning (CASEL; quoted in Gerszberg, n.d., ¶ 10). Emotional regulation, identifying one's emotional state and that of others, and cultivating agency are all crucial dimensions of emotional well-being.

What emotional wellness techniques have you used in your classroom? Work with colleagues to develop a list of ideas that are developmentally appropriate for your students.

TECHNIQUE	BRIEF DEFINITION	YOUR IDEAS
Guided breathing	Students perform exercises that regulate breathing, especially those that encourage deeper and slower breathing rates.	
Guided imagery	Students close their eyes and listen to a narration of a story meant to evoke a calm place, such as a beach, or an image, such as fish swimming.	
Sensory experiences	Students receive auditory prompts such as soothing music or other pleasant sounds, or experiences involving a pleasing smell or texture.	

INVEST IN A TRAUMA-SENSITIVE DESIGN IN THE CLASSROOM

As discussed in the Introduction, the impact of trauma, whether acute, chronic, or complex, takes a toll on the learning lives of children. In no way do we position the Tier 1 social-emotional learning efforts described in this playbook as being sufficient for addressing all the needs of young people experiencing trauma. To do so requires a system of specialized supports that may involve counselors, social workers, and outside agencies. However, "acknowledging that trauma is sitting in the classroom *is* transformational teaching" because you are adopting the proactive stance of acknowledging we might not ever know who has faced trauma (Romero et al., 2018, p. 65). In that sense, it doesn't matter. Let's make sure that our classrooms are trauma-sensitive to begin with.

We distinguish *trauma-informed* from *trauma-sensitive* to acknowledge that schools typically offer a narrower segment of mental health and social services and have less capacity to deliver direct services (Cole et al., 2013). A trauma-sensitive classroom and school seek to provide best practices for all students in an emotionally and psychologically safe environment (Fisher et al., 2019). Investment in teacher-student and peer relationships, prosocial skills, and emotional regulation are all part of your investment in proactively developing a trauma-sensitive classroom.

However, one overlooked element is in classroom design. It speaks to the notion that there are three "teachers" (interaction sources) in every classroom:

1. The relationship with the adults in the room

2. Relationships with peers

3. The relationship with the physical environment (Malaguzzi, 1984)

With this in mind, we redesigned classrooms at the school where we work to reflect principles of the environmental design meant to soothe and reduce stressors. We looked to Designs for Dignity, an architectural design firm that works with nonprofits who work with vulnerable populations, and learned more about environmental triggers for some people experiencing trauma. We learned about sensory inputs such as loud noises, neon-bright colors, and harsh lighting. In addition, the spatial layout can be challenging for some. Hypervigilant children may feel threatened due to their inability to see the door, and others may desire to have a place to retreat to.

We didn't engage in lots of high-cost efforts. But it was surprisingly affordable to make some investments in classrooms. We partnered with classroom teachers and students to figure out what we could do. One of the first fixes had to do with color. We repainted classrooms in soft shades of blue, green, and lavender, replacing institutional-white walls. In addition, we got rid of the neon- and jewel-toned paper that many of us were fond of and used to decorate. These intense-value colors were replaced with more muted colors.

Since sudden loud noises can be a problem, we embarked on a project to get all the classrooms carpeted. Many already had been, but some still had concrete floors. Covering them reduced the overall noise, and teachers in those rooms remarked that the reduction in noise made it easier to hear. With a grant, we converted our old lights to environmentally friendly LED lights, which eliminated the flickering fluorescent lights.

We worked with teachers on resetting tables and chairs to improve visibility and reduce the number of seats that did not have a sightline to the door. Because the clutter of physical objects can provoke anxiety for some, we asked that overhead objects be kept to a minimum (some teachers liked to hang swirling student work displays from the ceiling). In addition, we gave each teacher a small budget to purchase a few plants, or pictures of ones, for those who didn't want to do additional upkeep. Collectively, these small design changes gave us the opportunity to strengthen the "third teacher" present in every classroom.

NOTE TO SELF

Make an environmental scan of your classroom or school office. Are there any small design tweaks you can make to improve your "third teacher"?

DESIGN ELEMENT	NOTES	POSSIBLE IMPROVEMENTS
Color (Too institutional? Too bright? Too dark?)		
Lighting (Harsh? Flickering?)		
Layout (Cluttered?)		
Noise (Too loud?)		
Visual interest (Positive messages, student work)		
Presence of nature (Plants, rocks, photographs)		

CASE IN POINT

Some families have raised concerns about teaching techniques in school for emotional well-being. Two parents from different families in Alicia Foster's ninth-grade algebra class have asked to meet with her and the school principal. They said that their children have reported that Ms. Foster uses breathing and guided imagery techniques in her class. One parent expressed that they are suspicious of what they call "West Coast woo-woo stuff" when "the teacher's job is to teach my kid algebra. Period."

Ms. Foster and her principal will be meeting with each of the parents the following afternoon. How would you advise them to proceed?

A COMMUNITY OF CARE IS NURTURED BY SCHOOLS

A schoolwide commitment to fostering a community of care magnifies and multiplies the efforts of individual educators. This is of vital importance in considering the *school climate*. The climate is a manifestation of the school's social and environmental context. School climate has a direct influence on the academic learning of its students, with an effect size of 0.44 (https://www.visiblelearningmetax.com/). The research on school climate includes several dimensions, including the orderly nature of its procedures, the quality of the curriculum, its leadership, and the achievement mentality of the school. Woven through studies of school climate is communication among staff. A community of caring means that we take care of all the members of the organization.

> The school climate is a manifestation of the school's social and environmental context.

COLLECTIVE RESPONSIBILITY

Do educators in your school accept responsibility for student learning? By that, we mean not only the students on a teacher's current roster but rather of all the students in the school? *Collective responsibility* is the product of the actions of the school. Learning Forward, a professional organization focused on educator development, defines collective efficacy across five dimensions (Hirsh, 2010, p. 2):

1. All staff members share a commitment to the success of each student.

2. We do not allow any single teacher to fail in their attempt to ensure the success of any one student.

3. Our students benefit from the wisdom and expertise of *all* teachers in a grade level or subject, rather than just their own teachers.

4. Our teachers feel a responsibility to share what is working in their classrooms with their colleagues.

5. Teachers with less experience realize that other teachers are invested in their success and the success of all students.

Collective responsibility is a feature of a positive school climate that is driven by the communication the staff has with one another. This can be expressed through professional learning communities (PLC), as one example. However, in practice, team meetings are labeled PLCs, ignoring the evidence that the entire school is a single professional learning community, while the team meetings are only one part of the logistics for promoting collective responsibility (Hord, 1997). In too many buildings, "PLC time" is strictly at the grade level or department level, with no opportunities for teams to ever come together as a single entity to discuss the work. In the absence of communication, it is unlikely that collective responsibility can ever emerge.

That's a shame because there is strong evidence that collective responsibility can impact the performance of students and teachers (Park et al., 2019). The researchers analyzed the mathematics achievement trajectory of 25,000 students as they moved from ninth grade through eleventh grade, as well as the 5,700 math teachers of these students. The researchers found that higher levels of collective responsibility, principal support, and professional learning communities correlated to higher math achievement scores, even when the socioeconomic and linguistic status of the students was held as a constant.

COMMUNICATION COMPETENCY

Although rarely discussed, loneliness among teachers undermines efforts to foster collective responsibility. In many cases, the loneliness of an individual is attributed to their personality without interrogating the health of the organizational climate (Kazuk, 2021). Loneliness among staff has been exacerbated by prolonged social isolation from one another due to remote and hybrid learning, as well as the continued uncertainties faced by each of us as we continue through the unsteadiness of the twin pandemics of disease and racism.

> Although rarely discussed, loneliness among teachers undermines efforts to foster collective responsibility.

Communication competency is an essential professional skill that educators need in order to exchange ideas, work through interpersonal problems, and proactively address emerging challenges. The relative emotional wellness of the individuals in an organization to communicate and interact socially is imperative and worthy of sustained attention (Erdil & Ertosun, 2011). Kazuk's 2021 study of the relationship between emotional loneliness, the organization's communication competency, and the school's climate found that the first two factors impacted the attitudes and behaviors needed in a healthy school climate. Schools with a robust community of care foster the communication competencies of their members to strengthen one another's emotional wellness.

CASE IN POINT

The emotional climate at Oakdale Middle School has been challenging this year. People seem to be physically and emotionally tired and discouraged. Even among the teacher-leaders at the school, there is a more negative tone to conversations. Principal Imani Turner is concerned that the school climate is suffering and wants to consider some organizational responses to support the classified and certificated staff at Oakdale Middle. Principal Turner is meeting with her administrative team, as well as the lead school counselor and the social worker, to formulate a more coherent response to the current situation. She also recognizes that attending to student wellness will be important for her staff. She knows them to be caring educators who are also carrying the emotional burden of their students' lives. Use what you have learned in this module to help the Oakdale team. What advice do you have for them in each of these categories?

Emotional Wellness for Staff	Emotional Wellness for Students
Physical Wellness for Staff	**Physical Wellness for Students**

....

The ultimate outcome of a schoolwide approach to social-emotional learning is that we develop a community of care. Reflect on the extent to which a community of care exists in your school.

Menu of Practices on a Community of Care

Use the traffic light scale to reflect on your current practices as they relate to fostering a community of care. What areas do you want to strengthen?

INDIVIDUAL OPPORTUNITIES	
I have a wellness plan tailored to my needs about physical activity, healthy eating, and/or sleep hygiene.	
I foster and maintain social connections to keep isolation at bay.	
I am able to set time aside for myself every day, even when it is just a short time.	
I invest time through actions regularly in my school and neighborhood community.	
I check in regularly to gauge my own emotions.	
STUDENT-LEVEL OPPORTUNITIES	
I promote and advocate for students' physical wellness at my school.	
I use or help others use integrated physical activity in academic instruction.	
I use or help others use brain breaks in the classroom.	
I use or help others use mindfulness activities to promote the academic and emotional learning of students.	
SCHOOL-LEVEL APPROACHES	
I actively engage in and take action to foster collective responsibility at my school.	
I apply communication competency principles in my interactions with colleagues and students.	

● What do I need to do to change my reds to yellows?

● Who can support me to turn my yellows into greens?

● How am I using my greens to positively contribute to the good of the whole?

NOTE TO SELF

What are your next steps? Think about the entire book and all the modules you have read. We intentionally organized this book into specific modules that address the social and emotional needs of humans and provided you with opportunities to take action and implement ideas. These occurred at the self, student, and school levels. At this point, we encourage you to summarize your next steps in each of these areas.

	SELF	STUDENTS	SCHOOL
What are my short-term, or more immediate, plans?			
What are my mid-range plans, perhaps over the next six months?			
What are my longer-range plans over the next year or two?			

online resources

Access resources, tools, and guides for this module at
resources.corwin.com/theselplaybook

FINAL THOUGHTS

The German poet Christian Morgenstern noted that "home is not where you live, but where you are understood." We strongly believe that under the best of circumstances, home is where you live *and* where you are understood. A home-like school is a place of welcome, a space where people are respected and nurtured to reach their aspirations. To create such an environment means that we must see social-emotional learning (SEL) as a layered system. We cannot serve our students best if we ignore the needs of the educators in the building. We cannot serve our students best if we are not ensuring family voice. And we cannot serve our students best if SEL remains in silos, with hardworking educators undermined by a lack of schoolwide investment in our vision as an organization and without coordination of effort.

> A home-like school is a place of welcome, a space where people are respected and nurtured to reach their aspirations.

An investment in our students' social and emotional learning is an investment in their academic learning—the data are clear on that point. But we must also create the time and devote the energy needed to learn as a school and as individuals. They are worth it. So are you.

REFERENCES

Aguilar, E. (2018). *Onward: Cultivating emotional resilience in educators.* Wiley.

Angus, R. (2020). Can strengths-based interventions be used to support the financial wellbeing of tertiary students in financial need during COVID19? *Journal of the Australian and New Zealand Student Services Association, 28*(2), 96–101.

Asher, J. J. (1969). The Total Physical Response approach to second language learning. *The Modern Language Journal, 53*(1), 3–17.

Balchut, C. (2021, December 7). Before meeting new people, give them your personal user manual. *The Unconventional Route.* https://www.theunconventionalroute.com/personal-user-manual/

Bandura, A. (1977). Self-efficacy: Toward a unifying theory of behavioral change. *Psychological Review, 84*(2), 191–215.

Bandura, A. (1986). *Social foundations of thought and action: A social cognitive theory.* Prentice Hall.

Bandura, A. (1993). Perceived self-efficacy in cognitive development and functioning. *Educational Psychologist, 28,* 117–148.

Bandura, A. (1997). *Self-efficacy: The exercise of control.* W. H. Freeman.

Bandura, A. (2000). Exercise of human agency through collective efficacy. *Current Directions in Psychological Science, 9*(3), 75–78. https://doi.org/10.1111/1467-8721.00064

Barton, E. E., & Smith, B. J. (2015). Advancing high-quality preschool inclusion: A discussion and recommendations for the field. *Topics in Early Childhood Special Education, 35*(2), 69–78.

Bedard, C., St. John, L., Bremer, E., Graham, J. D., & Cairney, J. (2019). A systematic review and meta-analysis on the effects of physically active classrooms on educational and enjoyment outcomes in school age children. *PLoS One, 14*(6), e0218633. https://doi.org/10.1371/journal.pone.0218633

Borrero, N., & Sanchez, G. (2017) Enacting culturally relevant pedagogy: Asset mapping in urban classrooms. *Teaching Education, 28*(3), 279–295. https://doi: 10.1080/10476210.2017.1296827

Boske, C., Osanloo, A., & Newcomb, W. S. (2017). Exploring empathy to promote social justice leadership in schools. *Journal of School Leadership, 27*(3), 361–391.

Bowen, J. (2021, October 21). *Why is it important for students to feel a sense of belonging in school?* https://ced.ncsu.edu/news/2021/10/21/why-is-it-important-for-students-to-feel-a-sense-of-belonging-at-school-students-choose-to-be-in-environments-that-make-them-feel-a-sense-of-fit-says-associate-professor-deleon-gra/

Brackett, M., & Frank, C. (2017, September 11). Four mindful back-to-school questions to build emotional intelligence. *Washington Post.* https://www.washingtonpost.com/news/parenting/wp/2017/09/11/a-mindful-start-to-the-school-year-four-back-to-school-questions-to-build-emotional-intelligence/?noredirect=on&utm_term=.330035371ecc

Brackett, M. A., Bailey, C. S., Hoffmann, J. D., & Simmons, D. N. (2019). RULER: A theory-driven, systemic approach to social, emotional, and academic learning. *Educational Psychologist, 54*(3), 144–161.

Brackett, M. A., Floman, J. L., Ashton-James, C., Cherkasskiy, L., & Salovey, P. (2013). The influence of teacher emotion on grading practices: A preliminary look at the evaluation of student writing. *Teachers & Teaching, 19*(6), 634–646.

Brown, D. W., Anda, R. F., Felitti, V. J., Edwards, V. J., Malarcher, A. M., Croft, J. B., & Giles, W. H. (2010). Adverse childhood experiences are associated with the risk of lung cancer: A prospective cohort study. *BMC Public Health, 10,* 20. https://doi.org/10.1186/1471-2458-10-20

Brown, G. T. L., & Harris, L. R. (2014). The future of self-assessment in classroom practice: Reframing self-assessment as a core competency. *Frontline Learning Research, 3,* 22–30. https://doi.org/10.14786/flr.v2i1.24

Bryk, A. S. (2010). Organizing Schools for Improvement. *Phi Delta Kappan, 91*(7), 23–30.

Bryk, A. S., & Schneider, B. (2002). *Trust in schools: A core resource for improvement.* Russell Sage Foundation.

Bryk, A. S., Sebring, P. B., Allensworth, E., Luppescu, S., & Easton, J. Q. (2010). *Organizing schools for improvement: Lessons from Chicago.* University of Chicago Press.

CASEL. (n.d.a). *CASEL program guide.* pg.casel.org

CASEL. (n.d.b). *What is the CASEL framework?* https://casel .org/fundamentals-of-sel/what-is-the-casel-framework

Centers for Disease Control and Prevention. (2018). *Strategies for classroom physical activity in schools.* Centers for Disease Control and Prevention, U.S. Departtment of Health and Human Services. https://www.cdc.gov/ healthyschools/physicalactivity/pdf/classroompastrate gies_508.pdf

Centers for Disease Control and Prevention. (n.d.a). About the CDC-Kaiser ACE study. https://www.cdc .gov/violenceprevention/aces/about.html?CDC_AA_ refVal=https%3A%2F%2Fwww.cdc.gov%2Fviolen ceprevention%2Facestudy%2Fabout.html

Centers for Disease Control and Prevention. (n.d.b). *Adverse childhood experiences (ACEs).* Adverse Childhood Experiences (ACEs) (cdc.gov)

Cherry, K. (2020). Self efficacy and why believing in your-self matters. *Very Well Mind.* https://www.verywellmind .com/what-is-self-efficacy-2795954

Chou, C. Y., & Chang, C. H. (2021). Developing adaptive help-seeking regulation mechanisms for different help-seeking tendencies. *Educational Technology & Society, 24*(4), 54–66.

Clifton, D. O., & Harter, J. K. (2003). Investing in strengths. In K. S. Cameron, J. E. Dutton, & R. E. Quinn (Eds.), *Positive organizational scholarship: Foundations of a new discipline* (pp. 111–121). Berrett-Kohler.

Cohn-Vargas, B., Kahn, A. C., & Epstein, A. (2020). *Identity safe classrooms, grades 6–12.* Corwin.

Cole, S. F., Eisner, A., Gregory, M., & Ristuccia, J. (2013). *Helping traumatized children learn: Creating and advocating for trauma-sensitive schools.* Boston, MA: Massachusetts Advocates for Children.

Collaborative for Academic, Social, and Emotional Learning. (2021). *2011 to 2021: Ten years of social and emotional learning in US school districts: Elements for long-term sustainability of SEL.* https://casel.s3.us-east-2.ama zonaws.com/CDI-Ten-Year-Report.pdf

Coopersmith, S. (1967). *The antecedents of self esteem.* W. H. Freeman and Company.

Corwin Visible Learning Plus. (n.d.). *Visible Learning Meta^X global research database.* https://www.visiblelearning- metax.com/

Costa, A. L., & Garmston, R. J. (2015). *Cognitive coaching: Developing self-directed leaders and learners* (3rd ed.). Rowman & Littlefield.

Crockett, L. (2019). 6 ways of building student confidence through your practice. *Future Focused Learning.* https://blog.futurefocusedlearning.net/building -student-confidence-6-ways

Davidson, K., & Case, M. (2018). Building trust, elevating voices, and sharing power in family partnership. *Phi Delta Kappan, 99*(6), 49–53.

Davies, K., Lane, A., Devonport, T., & Scott, J. (2010). Validity and reliability of a Brief Emotional Intelligence Scale (BEIS-10), *Journal of Individual Differences, 31,* 198–208.

Davis-Bowman, J. (2021). African American child and adolescent academic help-seeking: A scoping review. *Education & Urban Society, 53*(1), 42–67.

Dimant, E. (2019). Contagion of pro- and anti-social behavior among peers and the role of social proximity. *Journal of Economic Psychology, 73,* 66–88.

Dockray, H. (2019). Self-care isn't enough. We need community care to thrive. *Mashable.* https://mashable.com/ article/community-care-versus-self-care

Duke University. (2022). How can I support student wellbeing? *Duke Flexible Teaching.* https://flex teaching.li.duke.edu/a-guide-to-course-design/how-can -i-support-student-well-being/

Durlak, J. A., Weissberg, R. P., & Pachan, M. (2010). A meta-analysis of after-school programs that seek to promote personal and social skills in children and adolescents. *American Journal of Community Psychology, 45,* 294–309.

Eisenberg, N., Eggum-Wilkens, N. D., & Spinrad, T. L. (2015). The development of prosocial behavior. In D. A. Schroeder, & W. G. Graziano (Eds.), *Oxford library of psychology. The Oxford handbook of prosocial behavior* (pp. 114–136). Oxford University Press.

Elliott, K. W., Elliott, J. K., & Spears, S. G. (2018). Teaching on empty. *Principal, 98*(2), 28–29.

Ellis, W. R., & Dietz, W. H. (2017). A new framework for addressing adverse childhood and community experiences: The building community resilience model. *Academic Pediatrics, 17*(7S), S86–S93. https://doi.org/ 10.1016/j.acap.2016.12.011

Ells, R. J. (2011). *Meta-analysis of the relationship between collective teacher efficacy and student achievement* [Unpublished doctoral dissertation]. Loyola University of Chicago.

Elmer, J. (2019). Not sure what to say to someone with depression? Here are seven ways to show support. *Healthline.* https://www.healthline.com/health/what-to -say-tosomeone-with-depression

Entrepreneur. (n.d.). *Branding.* https://www.entrepreneur .com/encyclopedia/branding

Erdil, Ö., & Ertosun, Ö. G. (2011). The relationship between social climate and loneliness in the workplace and effects on employee well-being. *Procedia Social and Behavioral Sciences, 24,* 505–525.

Eurich, T. (2018). What self-awareness really is and how to cultivate it. *Harvard Business Review.* https://hbr .org/2018/01/what-self-awareness-really-is-and-how -to-cultivate-it

Figley, C. R. (2002). Compassion fatigue: Psychotherapists' chronic lack of self care. *Journal of Clinical Psychology, 58*(11), 1433–1441.

Fisher, D., Frey, N., & Savitz, R. S. (2019). *Teaching hope and resilience for students experiencing trauma: Creating safe and nurturing classrooms for learning.* Teachers College Press.

Fisher, D., Smith, D., & Frey, N. (2020). *Teacher credibility and collective efficacy.* Corwin.

Frey, N. (2010). Home is not where you live, but where they understand you. In K. Dunsmore & D. Fisher (Eds.), *Bringing literacy home* (pp. 42–52). International Reading Association.

Galvin, B. M., Randel, A. E., Collins, B. J., & Johnson, R. E. (2018). Changing the focus of locus (of control): A targeted review of the locus of control literature and agenda for future research. *Journal of Organizational Behavior, 39*, 8200–833.

Gerszberg, C. O. (n.d.). Best practices for bringing mindfulness into schools. *Mindful.* https://www.mindful.org/mindfulness-in-education/

Goddard, R. D. (2003). Relational networks, social trust, and norms: A social capital perspective on students' chances of academic success. *Educational Evaluation & Policy Analysis, 25*(1), 59–74.

Goddard, R. D., Hoy, W. K., & Woolfolk Hoy, A. (2004). Collective efficacy beliefs: Theoretical developments, empirical evidence, and future directions. *Educational Researcher, 33*(3), 3–13.

Gonzalez, J. (2014). Know your terms: Holistic, analytic, and single-point rubrics. *Cult of Pedagogy.* www.cultofpedagogy.com/holistic-analytic-single-point-rubrics

Goodman, L. (2001). A tool for learning: Vocabulary self-awareness. In C. Blanchfield (Ed.), *Creative vocabulary: Strategies for teaching vocabulary in grades K-12* (p. 46). San Joaquin Valley Writing Project. Used with permission.

Gordon, T. (2003). *Teacher effectiveness training: The program proven to help teachers bring out the best in students of all ages.* Three Rivers Press.

Hardcastle, K., Bellis, M. A., Ford, K., Hughes, K., Garner, J., & Ramos Rodriguez, G. (2018). Measuring the relationships between adverse childhood experiences and educational and employment success in England and Wales: Findings from a retrospective study. *Public Health, 165*, 106–116.

Hattie, J. (2012). *Visible learning for teachers: Maximizing impact on learning.* Routledge.

Hattie, J., Fisher, D., Frey, N., & Clarke, S. (2021). *Collective student efficacy: Developing independent and interdependent learners.* Corwin.

Heller, R. (2017). On the science and teaching of emotional intelligence: An interview with Marc Brackett. *Phi Delta Kappan, 98*(6), 20–24.

Herman, D. B., Susser, E. S., Struening, E. L., & Link, B. L. (1997). Adverse childhood experiences: Are they risk factors for adult homelessness? *American Journal of Public Health, 87*, 249–255.

Hirsh, S. (2010). Collective responsibility makes all teachers the best. *Teachers Teaching Teachers, 6*(1). https://learningforward.org/leading-teacher/september-2010-vol-6-no-1/collective-responsibility-makes-all-teachers-the-best

Hord, S. M. (1997). *Professional learning communities: Communities of continuous inquiry and improvement.* Austin, TX: Southwest Educational Development Laboratory.

Hoy, W. K., Sweetland, S. W., & Smith, P. A. (2002). Toward an organizational model of achievement in high schools: The significance of collective efficacy. *Education Administration Quarterly, 38*(1), 77–93.

Hoy, W. K., & Tschannen-Moran, M. (2003). The conceptualization and measurement of faculty trust in schools: The omnibus T-Scale. In W. K. Hoy & C. G. Miskel (Eds.), *Studies in leading and organizing schools* (181–208). Information Age.

Identify Safe Classrooms. (n.d.). *Components of identify safety.* http://www.identitysafeclassrooms.com/more-about-identity-safety

Immordino-Yang, M. H., Christodoulou, J. A., & Singh, V. (2012). Rest is not idleness: Implications of the brain's default mode for human development and education. *Perspectives on Psychological Science, 7*(4), 352–364.

Jones, S., Brush, K., Bailey, K., Brion-Meisels, G., McIntyre, J., Kahn, J., Nelson, B., & Stickle, L. (2017). *Navigating SEL from the inside out: Looking inside and across 25 leading SEL programs: A practical resource for schools and OST providers: Elementary school focus.* Harvard Graduate School of Education and the Wallace Foundation. http://www.wallacefoundation.org/knowledge-center/Documents/Navigating-Social-and-Emotional-Learning-from-the-Inside-Out.pdf

Josh Meah & Company. (2019). *A simple marketing plan that works for most schools.* https://www.joshmeah.com/blog/a-basic-school-marketing-plan-for-all-schools

Kapur, M. (2016). Examining productive failure, productive success, unproductive failure, and unproductive success in learning. *Educational Psychologist, 51*(2), 289–299.

Kazuk, E. (2021). The predictive level of teachers' communication competencies and perceptions of school climate for loneliness at school. *International Online Journal of Educational Sciences, 13*(3), 722–739.

Kennedy, B. L., & Soutullo, O. (2018). "We can't fix that": Deficit thinking and the exoneration of educator responsibility for teaching students placed at a disciplinary alternative school. *Journal of At-Risk Issues, 21*(1), 11–23.

Keyes, T. S. (2019). A qualitative inquiry: Factors that promote classroom belonging and engagement among high school students. *School Community Journal, 29*(1), 171–200.

Kuypers, L. (2013). The zones of regulation: A framework to foster self-regulation. *Sensory Integration, 36*(4), 1–3.

Lee, C. K. J., & Huang, J. (2021). The relations between students' sense of school belonging, perceptions of school kindness and character strength of kindness. *Journal of School Psychology, 84*, 95–108.

Levine, E. (2007). *Henry's freedom box: A true story from the Underground Railroad.* Scholastic.

Livingstone, K. M., & Srivastava, S. (2012). Up-regulating positive emotions in everyday life: Strategies, individual differences, and associations with positive emotion and well-being. *Journal of Research in Personality, 46*, 504–526.

Maddux, J. E. (2013). *Self-efficacy, adaptation, and adjustment: Theory, research, and application.* Springer.

Maddux, J. E., & Meier, L. J. (1995). Self-efficacy and depression. In J. E. Maddux (Ed.), *Self-efficacy, adaptation, and adjustment* (pp. 143–169). Springer.

Malaguzzi, L. (1984). *When the eye jumps over the wall: Narratives of the possible.* Regione Emilia Romagna, Comune di Reggio Emilia.

Martín, R. K., & Santiago, R. S. (2021). Reduced emotional intelligence in children aged 9–10 caused by the COVID-19 pandemic lockdown. *Mind, Brain & Education, 15*(4), 269–272.

Maslow, A. (1954). *Motivation and personality.* Harper.

Massar, K., & Malmberg, R. (2017). Exploring the transfer of self-efficacy: Academic self-efficacy predicts exercise and nutrition self-efficacy. *Revista de Psicología Social, 32*(1), 108–135. https://doi.org/10.1080/02134748.2016.12 48026

Matsumoto, D., Frank, M. G., & Hwang, H. S. (2012). *Nonverbal communication: Science and applications.* Sage.

Mayer, J. D., & Salovey, P. (1997). What is emotional intelligence? In P. Salovey & D. J. Sluyter (Eds.), *Emotional development and emotional intelligence: Educational implications.* Basic Books.

Mayo Clinic Staff. (2020). *Anger management: 10 tips to tame your temper.* www.mayoclinic.org/healthy-lifestyle/ adult-health/in-depth/anger-management/art-20045434

McCawley, P. (n.d.). *The logic model for program planning and evaluation.* University of Idaho. www.cals.uidaho .edu/edcomm/pdf/CIS/CIS1097.pdf.

Merrick, M. T., Ports, K. A., Ford, D. C., Afifi, T. O., Gershoff, E. T., & Grogan-Kaylor, A. (2017). Unpacking the impact of adverse childhood experiences on adult mental health. *Child Abuse & Neglect, 69*, 10–19. https:// doi.org/10.1016/j.chiabu.2017.03.016

Mikami, A. Y., Griggs, M. S., Reuland, M., & Gregory, A. (2012). Teacher practices as predictors of children's classroom social preference. *Journal of School Psychology, 50*(1), 95–111.

Mind Tools. (n.d.). *Active listening.* https://www.mindtools .com/CommSkll/ActiveListening.htm

Minero, E. (2016, October 4). 4 steps of student self-assessment. *Edutopia.* https://www.edutopia.org/prac tice/mastering-self-assessment-deepening-indepen dent-learning-through-arts

Morin, A. (2021, October 25). *Impulse control techniques that work for children.* www.verywellfamily.com/ ways-to-teach-children-impulse-control-1095035

Murphey, D., & Sacks, V. (2019, Summer). *Supporting students with adverse childhood experiences: How educators and schools can help.* https://www.aft.org/ae/ summer2019/murphey_sacks

National Center on Safe Supportive Learning Environments. (n.d.). Tips for promoting positive peer-to-peer relationships. https://safesupportivelearning.ed.gov/sites/ default/files/Mod-2-Handout-4-508.pdf

National Scientific Council on the Developing Child. (2014). Excessive stress disrupts the architecture of the developing brain: Working paper 3. https://devel-opingchild.harvard.edu/wp-content/uploads/2005/05/ Stress_Disrupts_Architecture_Developing_Brain-1.pdf

New Economics Foundation. (2012). *Measuring wellbeing: A guide for practitioners.* Author.

Newberry, M., Sanchez, L. O., & Clark, S. K. (2018). Interactional dimensions of teacher change: A case study of the evolution of professional and personal relationships. *Teacher Education Quarterly, 45*(4), 29–50.

Nottingham, J. (2007). Exploring the learning pit. *Teaching Thinking and Creativity, 8*(23), 64–68.

Nottingham, J. (2017). *The learning challenge: How to guide your students through the learning pit to achieve deeper understanding.* Corwin.

Paley, V. G. (1993). *You can't say you can't play.* Harvard University Press.

Panadero, E., Jonsson, A., & Botella, J. (2017). Effects of self-assessment on self-regulated learning and self-efficacy: Four meta-analyses. *Educational Research Review, 22*, 74–98.

Paris, D., & Alim, S. (2017). *Culturally sustaining pedagogies: Teaching and learning for justice in a changing world.* Teachers College Press.

Park, J. H., Lee, I. H., & Cooc, N. (2019). The role of school-level mechanisms: How principal support, professional learning communities, collective responsibility, and group-level teacher expectations affect student achievement. *Educational Administration Quarterly, 55*(5), 742–780.

Patrick, H., Knee, C. R., Canevello, A., & Lonsbary, C. (2007). The role of need fulfillment in relationship functioning and well-being: A self-determination theory perspective. *Journal of Personality and Social Psychology, 92*(3), 434–457.

Penn State Wiki Spaces. (n.d.). *Self-efficacy and social cognitive theories.* https://wikispaces.psu.edu/display/ PSYCH484/7.+Self-Efficacy+and+Social+Cognitive+ Theories

Peterson, C., Park, N., & Seligman, M. E. P. (2005). Assessment of character strengths. In G. P. Koocher, J. C. Norcross, & S. S. Hill III (Eds.), *Psychologists' desk reference* (2nd ed., pp. 93–98). Oxford University Press.

Pipas, C. F., & Pepper, E. (2021). Building community well-being through emotional intelligence and cognitive reframing: With communities facing so much unrest, here are two skills you can apply to help promote healing. *Family Practice Management, 28*(1), 23–26.

Plutchik, R. (2001). The nature of emotions. *American Scientist, 89,* 344–350.

Plutchik, R. (2002). *Emotions and Life: Perspectives from psychology, biology, and evolution.* American Psychological Association.

Protheroe, N. (2008, May/June). Teacher efficacy: What is it and does it matter? *Principal,* 42–45.

Rath, T., & Conchie, B. (2009). *Strengths-based leadership: Great leaders, teams and why people follow.* Gallup Press.

Redmond, B. F. (2010). *Self-efficacy theory: Do I think that I can succeed in my work? Work attitudes and motivations.* The Pennsylvania State University, World Campus.

Rogers, E. (1962/2003). *Diffusion of innovation* (5th ed.). Simon and Schuster.

Romero, V. E., Robertson, R., & Warner, A. (2018). *Building resilience in students impacted by adverse childhood experiences.* Corwin.

Rotter, J. B. (1954). *Social learning and clinical psychology.* Prentice-Hall.

Ryan, A. M., Patrick, H., & Shim, S. (2005). Differential profiles of students identified by their teacher as having avoidant, appropriate, or dependent help-seeking tendencies in the classroom. *Journal of Educational Psychology, 97*(2), 275–285.

Ryan, A. M., & Shin, H. (2011). Help-seeking tendencies during early adolescence: An examination of motivational correlates and consequences for achievement. *Learning & Instruction, 21*(2), 247–256.

Ryan, R., & Deci, E. (2000). Self-determination theory and the facilitation of intrinsic motivation, social development, and well-being. *American Psychologist, 55*(1), 68–78.

Sacks, V., Murphey, D., & Moore, K. (2014). *Adverse childhood experiences: National and state-level prevalence.* Child Trends.

Salloum, S., Goddard, R., & Larsen, R. (2017). Social capital in schools: A conceptual and empirical analysis of the equity of its distribution and relation to academic development. *Teachers College Record, 119,* 1–29.

Salovey, P., & Mayer, J. D. (1990). Emotional intelligence. *Imagination, Cognition and Personality, 9,* 185–211.

Sanders, B. (2020, December 7). The power of social and emotional learning: Why SEL is more important than ever. *Forbes.* https://www.forbes.com/sites/forbesnonprofitcouncil/2020/12/07/the-power-of-social-and-emotional-learning-why-sel-is-more-important-than-ever/?sh=7d539b247a29

Satterfield, J. M. (2017). *The iceberg: Visible and hidden identity.* https://www.thegreatcoursesdaily.com/visible-and-hidden-identity/

Schutte, N. S., & Malouff, J. M. (2019). The impact of signature character strengths interventions: A meta-analysis. *Journal of Happiness Studies, 20,* 1179–1196.

Seligman, M., & Csikszenzentmihalyi, M. (2000). Positive psychology: An introduction. *American Psychologist, 55*(1), 5–14.

Shapiro, S. (2007). Revisiting the teachers' lounge: Reflections on emotional experiences and teacher identity. *Teaching and Teacher Identity, 6,* 616–621.

Sinanis, T., & Sanfelippo, J. (2015). *The power of branding: Telling your school's story.* Corwin.

Singleton, G. E. (2015). *Courageous conversations about race: A field guide for achieving equity in schools* (2nd ed.). Corwin.

Six Seconds. (n.d.). *Emotoscope feeling chart.* www.6seconds.org/free-emotoscope-feeling-chart

Smith, D., Fisher, D., & Frey, N. (2021). *Removing labels, grades K-12: 40 techniques to disrupt negative expectations about students and schools.* Corwin.

Smith, D., Frey, N., & Fisher, D. (2022). *The restorative practices playbook: Tools for transforming discipline in school.* Corwin.

Stamm, B. H. (2010). *The concise ProQOL manual* (2nd Ed.). ProQOL.org.

Steele, C. M., & Aronson, J. (1995). Stereotype threat and the intellectual test performance of African Americans. *Journal of Personality and Social Psychology, 69,* 797–811.

Steele, D. M., & Cohn-Vargas, B. (2013). *Identity safe classrooms: Places to belong and learn.* Corwin.

Style, E. J. (2014). Curriculum as encounter: Selves and shelves. *English Journal, 103*(5), 67–74.

Tajfel, H. (1979). Individuals and groups in social psychology. *British Journal of Social and Clinical Psychology, 18*(2), 183–190.

Tigchelaar, T. (n.d.). *How to create a successful school branding strategy.* https://www.finalsite.com/blog/p/~board/b/post/how-to-create-a-successful-school-branding-strategy-1596812941944

Toren, N. K., & Seginer, R. (2015). Classroom climate, parental educational involvement, and student school functioning in early adolescence: A longitudinal study. *Social Psychology of Education, 18*(4), 811–827.

Toshalis, E., & Nakkula, M. J. (2012). *Motivation, engagement, and student voice: The students at the center series.* Jobs for the Future. https://www.howyouthlearn.org/pdf/Motivation%20Engagement%20Student%20Voice_0.pdf

Transforming Education. (2020). *Introduction to self-management.* https://transformingeducation.org/resources/introduction-to-self-management/

Tschannen-Moran, M., & Hoy, A. W. (n.d.). *Research tools.* https://wmpeople.wm.edu/site/page/mxtsch/researchtools

Tschannen-Moran, M., & Woolfolk Hoy, A. (2001). Teacher efficacy: Capturing an elusive construct. *Teaching and Teacher Education, 17*(7), 783–805.

Tschannen-Moran, M., Woolfolk Hoy, A., & Hoy, W. K. (1998). Teacher efficacy: Its meaning and measure. *Review of Educational Research, 68,* 202–248.

Valencia, R. R. (2010). *Dismantling contemporary deficit thinking: Educational thought and practice.* Routledge.

Valente, S., Monteiro, A. P., & Lourenço, A. A. (2019). The relationship between teachers' emotional intelligence and classroom discipline management. *Psychology in the Schools, 56*(5), 741–750.

Van der Kolk, B. (2015). *The body keeps the score: Brain, mind, and body in the healing of trauma.* Penguin.

Veerman, G. J., & Denessen, E. (2021). Social cohesion in schools: A non-systematic review of its conceptualization and instruments. *Cogent Education, 8*(1). https://doi.org/10.1080/2331186X.2021.1940633

VIA Institute on Character. (n.d.). *The 24 character strengths.* https://www.viacharacter.org/character-strengths

Victoria Department of Education and Early Childhood Development. (2012). *Strength-based approach: A guide to writing transition and learning and development statements.* www.education.vic.gov.au/earlylearning/transitionschool

Vig, K. D., Paluszek, M. M., Asmundson, G. J. G. (2020). ACEs and physical health outcomes. In G. J. G. Asmundson & T. O. Afifi (Eds.), *Adverse childhood experiences: Using evidence to advance research, practice, policy, and prevention* (pp. 71–90). Academic Press.

Walton, G. E., & Hibbard, D. R. (2019). Exploring adults' emotional intelligence and knowledge of young children's social-emotional competence: A Pilot Study. *Early Childhood Education Journal, 47*(2), 199–206.

Warren, C. A. (2018). Empathy, teacher dispositions, and preparation for culturally responsive pedagogy. *Journal of Teacher Education, 69*(2), 169–183.

Waters, L. (2017). *The strength switch: How the new science of strength-based parentings can help your child and your teen to flourish.* Avery.

Wentzel, K. R., Jablansky, S., & Scalise, N. R. (2021). Peer social acceptance and academic achievement: A meta-analytic study. *Journal of Educational Psychology, 113*(1), 157–180.

WHO-5 Well-Being Index. (1998). *Psychiatric research unit WHO collaborating centre in mental health.* Author.

Willms, J. D. (2013). *Student engagement at school: A sense of belonging and participation.* Organisation for Economic Co-operation and Development.

Wlodkowski, R. J., & Ginsberg, M. B. (1995). A framework for culturally responsive teaching. *Educational Leadership, 53*, 17–21.

World Health Organization. (2004). *Promoting mental health: Concepts, emerging evidence, and practice. Summary report.* Author.

Y Studios. (2020). *What factors really influence identity?* https://ystudios.com/insights-people/influence-on-identity

Yeh, C. J., Borrero, N. E., Tito, P., & Petaia, L. S. (2014). Intergenerational stories of "othered" youth through insider cultural knowledge and community assets. *The Urban Review, 46*, 225–243.

Your Therapy Source. (2019, August 29). *Student strengths in the classroom: Find the positive.* https://www.yourtherapysource.com/blog1/2019/08/26/student-strengths-in-the-classroom-2/

Zaehringer, J., Jennen-Steinmetz, C., Schmahl, C., Ende, G., & Paret, C. (2020). Psychophysiological effects of down-regulating negative emotions: Insights from a meta-analysis of healthy adults. *Frontiers of Psychology, 11*(470). https://doi.org/10.3389/fpsyg.2020.00470

Zhu, M., Liu, Q., Fu, Y., Yang, T., Zhang, X., & Shi, J. (2018) The relationship between teacher self-concept, teacher efficacy and burnout. *Teachers and Teaching, 24*(7), 788–801. https://doi.org/10.1080/13540602.2018.1483913

Zimmerman, B. J., & Moylan, A. R. (2009). Self-regulation: Where metacognition and motivation intersect. In D. J. Hacker, J. Dunlosky, & A. C. Graesser (Eds.), *Handbook of metacognition in education* (pp. 299–315). Routledge.

INDEX

School
  branding, 59–60
  climate, 157, 171–172
  community, 27, 94–95, 113–114, 162
  systems, 122–123
Self-assessment, 34, 62, 91, 118, 127,
    135, 142–143, 150, 174
Self-awareness, 15, 42, 67–72, 74–75, 85, 91, 97, 127
Self-care, 154–155
Self-confidence, 34
Self-control, 8, 67, 69, 80
Self-determination, 12–15, 19, 34
Self-efficacy, 123–125, 127, 142, 145
Self-esteem, 49, 122–123
Self-knowledge, 16, 43, 62
Self-management, 15, 42, 68–69, 80–81,
    85, 88, 97, 127
Self-regulation, 16, 90, 133, 136, 142, 166
Smith, D., 38, 45, 47, 49, 73, 80
Social capital, 5, 13, 15, 27–28, 32, 34, 86, 94
Social cohesion, 96–97, 103, 105
Social identities, 39–40, 54
Social interactions, 12, 39, 108–109
Social media, 60
Social skills, 20, 52, 55, 95, 103, 108–111, 118
Steele, D. M., 54
Stereotype threat, 20–22, 51, 136
Strengths-based approach, 10–13, 16,
    20, 24–25, 27, 30, 32–34
Student
  achievement, 72, 145
  efficacy, 133–134, 143, 150
  grouping, 106

study groups, 137
  success, 40, 55, 114
  voices, 51, 53, 115
Student profile, 112
Substance abuse, 4–5, 7, 106

Teacher actions, 49
Teacher credibility, 96–97, 103, 118
Teacher warmth, 52
Teachers' sense of efficacy scale, 128
Teacher-student relationships, 44, 94, 103
Toshalis, E., 115
Total physical response (TPR), 163
Traditions, family and cultural, 21–22
Trauma, 3, 7, 13, 38, 168
Trust, 27, 52, 59, 76–77, 94, 95, 96, 97–99,
    100–101, 104, 111, 115, 118, 124
Tschannen-Moran, M., 98, 128–129, 145

University of Chicago Lab Schools, 56
Up-regulation, 66–69

Values in Action Inventory of Strengths
    (VIA-IS), 16–17, 23
Visible Learning®, 7–8, 20, 71, 103, 111,
    162–163, 166, 171

Warwick-Edinburgh Mental Well-Being
    Scale (WEMWBS), 159
Wheel of emotions, 77
Woolfolk Hoy, A., 128

Yale Center for Emotional Intelligence, 85

CORWIN Fisher&Frey

" Every student deserves a great teacher—
not by chance, but by design. "

Read more from Fisher & Frey

Transform negative behavior into a teachable moment at your school, utilizing restorative practices that are grounded in relationships and a commitment to the well-being of others.

Rich with resources that support the process of parlaying scientific findings into classroom practice, this playbook offers all the moves teachers need to design learning experiences that work for all students.

Harnessing decades of Visible Learning® research, this easy-to-read, eye-opening guide details the six essential components of effective tutoring.

Catapult teachers beyond learning intentions to define clearly what success looks like for every student. This step-by-step playbook expands teacher understanding of how success criteria can be utilized to maximize student learning.

Disrupt the cycle of implicit bias and stereotype threat with 40 research-based, teacher-tested techniques; individual, classroom-based, and schoolwide actions; printables; and ready-to-go tools for planning and instruction.

Explore a new model of reading instruction that goes beyond teaching skills to fostering engagement and motivation. *Comprehension* is the structured framework you need to empower students to comprehend text and take action in the world.

To order your copies, visit corwin.com/FisherandFrey

CORWIN

Fisher & Frey

Bring the Fisher & Frey team to your school

Virtual and On-Site Professional Learning Services From Corwin

Work with a certified consultant for customized support on key initiatives:

- Distance Learning
- PLC+
- Teacher Clarity
- Balanced Literacy
- Close & Critical Reading
- Visible Learning® for Literacy
- Tutoring
- Social-Emotional Learning
- Restorative Practices

Douglas Fisher & Nancy Frey

CORWIN Fisher & Frey

FFN22294

Visit corwin.com/fisherfreyconsulting

A SAGE Publishing Company

Helping educators make the greatest impact

CORWIN HAS ONE MISSION: to enhance education through intentional professional learning.

We build long-term relationships with our authors, educators, clients, and associations who partner with us to develop and continuously improve the best evidence-based practices that establish and support lifelong learning.